Phenomenology and Art

JOSÉ ORTEGA Y GASSET

PHENOMENOLOGY
AND ART

TRANSLATED, WITH AN INTRODUCTION BY
PHILIP W. SILVER

W · W · NORTON & COMPANY · INC · New York

FIRST EDITION

Library of Congress Cataloging in Publication Data
Ortega y Gasset, José, 1883–1955.
    Phenomenology and art.
    Includes bibliographical references.
    CONTENTS: Autobiography and phenomenology: Preface
for Germans (1934).—Phenomenology and theory of knowledge:
Sensation, construction, and intuition (1913). On the concept of
sensation (1913). Consciousness, the object, and its three distances
(1916). [etc.]
    1. Phenomenology—Collected works. 2. Aesthetics—Collected
works. I. Title.
B4568.072E5 1975   196'.1   74–34144
ISBN 0–393–08714–X

1 2 3 4 5 6 7 8 9 0

Contents

Introduction

ALTHOUGH ESSAYS BY José Ortega y Gasset have been appearing in English since 1932, it still cannot be said that he needs no introduction to English-speaking audiences. Most readers are familiar with *The Revolt of the Masses* or *The Dehumanization of Art,* so it cannot be that his works do not travel well. At least when the subject in our universities is esthetics or the novel, no other contemporary philosopher comes so readily to mind. Yet this is precisely why Ortega needs a new introduction—because he *is* so familiar, because for so long he has been "already there."

With the renewed interest in phenomenology, a solution is now at hand. Ortega's problem with both his Spanish and his foreign readers has been that as an unclassifiable, vaguely philosophical essayist, he seemed to stand virtually alone, with no context to support or explain him. These essays will place Ortega where he belongs, in the mainstream of the phenomenological movement. Once there he can be seen to have been the first existential phenomenologist of all, adopting this position in 1913 when Husserl himself had only just published the first edition of his *Ideas.*

Thus the purpose of this new selection of essays is to place Ortega in his proper context and provoke his re-examination there. While at present many of his important essays are available in English, those translated here for the first time are absolutely essential for a complete—perhaps even a minimal—understanding of his work already in English.

Given this hermeneutic criterion of selection, the reader will no doubt be surprised at the obvious and profound homogeneity of the collection. And indeed it is no fortuitous event that the most philosophical of these essays deal with phenomenology, while those in esthetics are all in some sense phenomenological. Rather, this coherence faithfully mirrors several important and related facts about Ortega's work: (1) the phenomenology of Brentano and Husserl played a basic part in the genesis of his philosophy; (2) as a young man he felt it part of his mission as a Spanish philosopher to write an Esthetics; and (3) while he never wrote an Esthetics as such, because this vocation remained, those essays on the arts that he *did* write constitute (a) the clearest indication that he "overcame" Husserl, and (b) the surest index to the accomplishment of his philosophical program. This is why these papers on phenomenology, esthetics, and the arts are either explanatory, seminal, or exemplary.

I have placed the most helpful essay first. This "Preface" gives an historical account of the level at which his other writings must be read. As a piece of philosophical autobiography it gives a fairly detailed account of his relation to phenomenology, and is also an excellent preview of that transmutation of circumstance into doctrine and method so characteristic of all Ortega wrote. Without this "Preface" his first and most important book, *Meditations on Quixote* (1914), cannot be read in depth.

To assess the studies in Part II, it must be borne in mind that, like *Meditations*, they were written by "a professor of Philosophy *in partibus infidelium*" as he termed himself. But instead of popularizing, which in the Spain of 1913 could have had no meaning, Ortega, as a specialist in philosophy, reached out to specialists in other fields, to fellow intellectuals in Gramsci's directive and organizational sense. "Sensation, Construction, and Intuition," delivered at the Fourth Congress of the Spanish Association for the Advancement of Science, shows his interest in science to be that of a philosopher closer to Brentano and Husserl than to his own former neo-Kantian professors at Marburg. "On the Concept of Sensation" and "Consciousness, the Object, and Its Three Distances" are primarily expositions of phenomenology as it had appeared in print by 1916. Notice that the first of these studies is not uncritical, and that it breaks off abruptly just as it begins to touch on material that also appears in *Meditations*.

With the essays in Part III we reach the actual implementation of Ortega's philosophical program. "An essay in Esthetics" is a circumstantial piece from 1914, yet in the guise of a preface Ortega gives an explanation of metaphor that touches on the ontological status of the art object itself. Not only that, but when pressed in the right place, this essay opens to reveal a Brentanian critique of Husserl's transcendental-phenomenological reductions that demands comparison with Sartre's "The Transcendence of the Ego," published in 1936–37. "Esthetics on the Streetcar," an apparently offhand, scherzo piece, is a careful phenomenological account of the judgment of taste.

Part IV contains late studies on theatre and painting, less Sibylline than those in the previous section. Although Ortega never made available to his disciples a systematic philosophy in the traditional sense, by the time he finished *Meditations* in 1914 he had accomplished two things. First, he had resolved the dispute between skepticism and dogmatism, realism and idealism, with a thesis about a new ontological category called "human life." Second, he had evolved a phenomenological method with which to re-examine phenomena as diverse as the problem of Being and a picture frame, so as to uncover not their received meanings but those that derive from the deepest strata of "human life." As this thesis subsists in the late essays it is properly called Vital or Historical Reason, while the method, described at the end of "Reviving the Paintings," is spoken of as "a dialectic of real things." This leads, as these late studies make abundantly clear, to a genuine "phenomenology of origins," to a "finding of the Idea in the Hegelian sense," to use two apt expressions made current by Merleau-Ponty.

Today it is easier to see why Ortega was misunderstood by his peers, especially as an appropriate context for his work has only appeared in recent years. In Ortega's case, it is true, this incomprehension of his contemporaries was further aggravated by the Spanish Civil War: in the general diaspora he and his disciples scattered over the Spanish and English-speaking worlds. But even before the war three serious tactical errors had mitigated against his being understood: (1) References to his own philosophy were nearly always oblique. As late as 1924 he spoke of "a new philosophy" as though it were something anonymously generated by philosophy itself; (2) Although in 1925 he formally presented a program of phenomenological investigation based on the "intuition" and analysis of "human life," his misunderstood insistence on systematic thought, together with repeated promises of a magnum opus to come, left the impression that even by his own standards he had not "said" very much at all; (3) Actual presentations of his thesis and method were intentionally so circumstantial that they went unnoticed. A reference to *Meditations* will clarify this point. In essence what Ortega does there is to address three questions to Cervantes' novel: What is Spain?, What is a novel?, and What is Cervantes' way of dealing

with things?. But while the questions are clearly formulated, the answers are not. Ortega ties the questions of
what Spain and the novel are to Cervantes' way of dealing with things, and a description of this, the philosophical keystone of the matter, is postponed until a later
Meditation that was never written. What he does do in
Meditations is not so much expose his thesis as presuppose
it and then describe its genesis in his own life and that of
his country. Small wonder the book is imperfectly read
by Spaniards as a contribution to the national debate on
Spain, and by foreigners as a treatise on the novel.

Now, with this selection of essays in hand, English-
speaking readers have access to the necessary materials
for a more complete understanding of *Meditations, The
Dehumanization of Art,* and even *The Revolt of the
Masses.* When read by itself, *Meditations* may seem to
present, as one critic has observed, an "existentialist" version of certain of Kant's ideas. Once "An Essay in Esthetics" has been studied, however, both *Meditations* and
The Dehumanization of Art can be seen to be based less
on Kant than on Brentano and Husserl, and especially on
the former's descriptive and genetic psychology.

When the essays by Ortega available in English have
been read in the light of those collected here, it will be
an easier task to judge his originality and place him
within the phenomenological movement as a whole. If,
until now, we have only seen Ortega with Spanish eyes,
that is, as a popularizer of German ideas, it will come as
a therapeutic shock to discover that his first book presupposes as its philosophical thesis that same "primacy
of perception" on which Merleau-Ponty's reputation as
a philosopher is based.

Finally, whatever Ortega's place in the history of
philosophy, the authenticity of his vocation as regards
Spain cannot be doubted; for as it turns out his mission

was not to write the Esthetics he imagined as a young man in Marburg, nor even to naturalize Husserlian phenomenology in Spain, but rather to bring a new Spanish philosophy into being, by "thematizing" Cervantes' "way of looking at things."

PHILIP W. SILVER

Acknowledgments

I WISH TO THANK the philosopher's heirs and executors for permission to translate the essays published here. I also wish to thank Paulino Garagorri with whom I first discussed this project, Ed Duncan who did a first version of "Ensayo de estética a manera de prólogo" while a student at Oberlin College, and Paul de Man, to whom, if it were in my power, I would dedicate these translations.

P. S.

1 Autobiography and Phenomenology

Preface for Germans *

THIS IS really too much. . . . The state of affairs I refer
to is that my books have gone through edition after edition in Germany. Things cannot go on this way, at least
not without additional explanations, corrections, and clarification. That is why when one of the accomplices in
this event, the kind director of *Deutsche Verlags–Anstalt*, wrote me about a year ago that *The Theme of Our
Time* was out of print and he must immediately launch
a third edition, I begged him to hold up publication at
least until I could send him a revised text and a preface
written especially for my German readers. Since I wrote
it, some twelve years ago, I had had neither the time nor
the inclination to reread this book, and I harbored the
vague impression that for non-Spanish readers, who did
not know the rest of my work and my university lectures, it could only express the fundamental idea that it
contained in a very deficient way. Now, here is what
seems to me to be beyond bearing. It is all very well that
I never intended my books—we will soon see why—to be
translated into German, it is all very well, nonetheless,
that someone living at the time in Switzerland should decide years ago to publish this work so as to make it
available to a group of her friends who did not know
Spanish, but what is not to be borne is that this pleasantry
intended for an enthusiastic *coterie* should become a seri-

* This "preface" never appeared in Germany. Events in Mu-
nich in 1934 so disgusted Ortega that he forbade its publication
[Translator's Note].

ous public event in edition after edition. Because, while I do not have a particularly high regard for this book as a book, some of its ideas are very important to me and I must oppose their appearance before a large public of unknown people in this poorly articulated and defenseless way.

This informs the reader of at least one new fact, to wit: that up until now I have not been responsible for those books appearing in the windows of German bookstores. The guilty one—let us inform on her—is Helene Weyl, my translator, and her accomplice, Dr. Kipler, of *Deutsche Verlags—Anstalt*. Here is what I told the latter when I sent him the authorizatoin required by law. I laid on the translator and on him the entire responsibility for the venture. Since then, even at the risk of seeming discourteous, I have not written the editor again, so as not to make myself, in turn, an accomplice in the crime. Not until last year did I write asking him to hold up the new edition and promising him shortly corrections to the text and the small figurehead of a preface. But the bohemian existence I lead, the result of anything but a bohemian life, the result in fact of an excess of obligations and work, hard for a German to imagine since they belong to a nation in which work is more evenly distributed . . . (Do you think you work harder than we Southerners, than at least some of us do? How wrong you are! I have to be at the same time a university professor, a journalist, a writer, a politician, an active conversationalist at the cafe I frequent, a bullfighter, a "man of the world," a kind of parish priest, and I don't know what else. It is less easy to decide if this *polypragmosyne* is a good thing or not.) But my bohemian existence—I said—prevented me from keeping my promise on time and the editor—who has behaved in an exemplary way— now has complained to me in the gentlest fashion that I am hurting his prospects. Now then, the thought of hurting anyone frightens me. Naturally it surprises me a little that this poor thing that I am, a diminutive outcropping of the granite folds of one of the oldest mountains in the world—the Guadarrama range—could be prejudicial at a distance of thousands of miles to the interests of a fine person who lives in as pretty a city as Stuttgart. On the other hand, in the child's periphery of our being that stays with us all—the tender surface of the soul, that is, for its "first steps" are always childlike—that zone where vanity is active—and vanity is a remnant of childishness in maturity—this fact causes me no little foolish satisfaction. It makes me feel like saying to passers-by when I walk down the street: Do you know what? I am hurting the interests of a German publisher by not letting him bring out a new edition of my works. Yes, sir! I am! Imagine it!

Thus the need not to let my ideas appear undefended, together with the desire to repay the editor for the delight I have had in hurting his interests, has moved me to write this preface.

But the reader at this point, will be saying that these scruples and explanations over the unimportant fact of whether a book is published or not are out of proportion. Excuse me, reader! I don't agree. One of the things life has taught me is that nothing is a matter of indifference if one has a moderately clear view of reality: everything, even what seems least important, produces effects that either help or harm. The publication of my writing in German is either advantageous or it is harmful to the German reader or to me. *Tertium non datur.*

And, for the present, it is harmful for an author if his readers do not know him. When Goethe said that the written word is a substitute for the spoken word he said something much more profound than may at first appear. What he said was that finally, strictly and truly what we usually call "ideas," "thoughts," do not exist; they are an abstraction, an approximation. The reality is the idea, the thought of a certain man. Only when it is seen as coming from him, from the entirety of his life, only when it is viewed against the background of the entire landscape of his concrete existence, does an idea appear in its true light. When the idea refers to an especially abstract subject like mathematics, *practically speaking* it can be detached from the concrete man who thought it and imputed instead to that abstract person, the geometrician. But ideas whose referents are authentic realities cannot be separated from the man who conceived them; they cannot be understood unless we understand the man, unless we know *who* spoke them. Speech, the *logos*, is really no less than the specific reaction of an individual life. Therefore, there are, in fact, no arguments except those that take place man to man. Because conversely, an idea is always a rather crude instrument if its author does not take into account just whom he is saying it to. Speech, the *logos*, in its fundamental reality, is the most human of conversations, a *diálogos—διάλογος—argumentum hominis ad hominem*. Dialogue is the *logos* from the point of view of the *other*, the neighbor.

This is the clear and simple norm that has governed my writing since I was young. Every word says something—everyone knows this as he knows his own name—but, in addition, every word says something to someone—the professor, the German "Gelehrte," knows this as well as I do; however, cruel and overbearing, they tend to forget it.

If the reader analyzes what may have pleased him in my work, he will find that it lies simply in the fact that I am present in every sentence I write, with the timbre of my voice, gesturing, and that if he rests his finger on any one of my pages he will feel my heart beat. But if he analyzes further he will find the whole answer.

My presence in each of my utterances is not due to any more or less "brilliant" gift of mine, and much less—this would be unpleasant—to the fact that, like Chateaubriand, I put myself in what I write to force the reader to bump into me—you know I have hardly ever spoken of myself—*but just the opposite:* this effect is achieved because *I put the reader* in my writings to the degree that this is possible, I take him into account, make him feel that he is there for me, that I am concerned for his concrete, anguished, and rudderless self. He senses that a ghostly yet real hand rises from the page, one that touches his person, that wants to caress it—or instead, to give it a courteous shove.

My intention has been to return the book to the condition of dialogue.

In a humble attic in Marburg, in the heights of that steep city, the excellent Nicolai Hartmann was playing his 'cello. I listened. We were twenty-two or twenty-three. The insistently pathetic, almost manly melody of the 'cello soared and wheeled in the air like a swallow. Through the small window I watched it fall toward the city, on its hillside, and down into the valley where the River Lahn flows, singing always its nonsong.

Hartmann paused for a moment, his bow in the air, and, separated from the 'cello, the bow became for a moment the tiny bow of a savage, a pygmy. He said:

"You, dear Ortega, are an intellectual altruist."

And then he released that melodic swallow of his again, the one that nests in the blond womb of his 'cello, out of which he has brought forth four or five splendid books.

But this desire to take the reader's most concrete reality into account, this longing to take careful aim as I write, has the inconvenience of sharply limiting the field at which I may fire. As we will see in a moment, everything I have written until this preface was written *exclusively and ad hoc* for the people of Spain and Latin America who more or less know the outlines of my personal life as I know the intellectual and moral outlines of theirs. I have always tried not to write *urbi et orbi*. And now against my will and because of a friendly behest pages that were written for Spaniards and Argentinians of a certain period will be heard near the Black Forest, speaking German to Germans. Perhaps now my scruples, my concern and uneasiness are understandable. I spoke to Juan, I counted on him and on his knowing who spoke to him, and suddenly Juan is taken away and I find myself *saying the same thing* to Pedro, whom I had scarcely taken into account and who I am certain does not know me. My purpose has been neatly contravened. I find myself in the situation I detest most: I am an unknown speaking to an unknown. This is a complete abstraction.

It may be thought that because one takes into account a specific person one takes into account all mankind, and that since he is part of mankind the German reader will feel included in my writing. Again, reader, excuse me! I always try to comply with the rules of good breeding—like the most venerable of London clubmen—and I never allow myself to speak to anyone unless we have first been introduced. Well, I have never been introduced to that gentleman who goes by the name of Humanity. I don't know who he is, and to the extent that I have an inkling who he is, I have always tried to avoid him.

There is a story—no one is certain that it really occurred—about how, when Victor Hugo was the subject of a Jubilee, a grand party was given in his honor at the Elysée Palace, and representatives of every country imaginable were invited so they might pay him homage. The great poet stood there in the reception room with the solemn mein of a statue, one elbow resting on the mantelpiece. Before a large audience the representatives of the different nations followed one another in presenting their homage to France's poet. An usher announced them in a loud voice, one by one.

"Monsieur le représentant de l'Angleterre!"

And Victor Hugo, his voice a dramatic tremolo, his eyes raised upward, said:

"L'Angleterre! Ah, Shakespeare!"

The usher continued: "Monsieur le représentant de l'Espagne!"

And Victor Hugo: "L'Espagne! Ah, Cervantes!"

The usher: "Monsieur le représentant de l'Allemagne!"

And Victor Hugo: "L'Allemagne! Ah, Goethe!"

But then it was the turn of a small, squat, fattish gentleman with a graceless walk. The usher called out:

"Monsieur le représentant de la Mésopotamie!"

Victor Hugo, who until then had been at ease and sure of himself, seemed to waver. Anxiously his eyes made a great circle as though searching the entire universe for something he could not find. But then it was clear he had found it and once more felt in command of the situation. And in truth, with the same pathetic tones, with the same conviction as before, he replied to the rotund representative's homage with these words:

"La Mésopotamie! Ah, l'Humanité."

I tell this anecdote so as to declare, but without Victor Hugo's solemnity, that I have never written or spoken for Mesopotamia, and I have never addressed myself to Humanity.

2

Since my books were written for Spaniards and not for "humanity," their reading must require an adjustment of German eyes. Only that benevolence Germans know how to show, only that heartfelt generosity they can offer when they want—*especially when they are caught off guard and show themselves as they really are*—could have made up for what was lacking in my books from their point of view. Nevertheless if I am to consent to their continued publication in German, a formal readjustment will be absolutely necessary. And this will entail my explaining to readers in Germany what my books are and in the process who I am.

And the first thing I ought to say about my books is that properly speaking they are not books at all. To a great extent my writings are solely, simply, and humbly articles published in the most widely read newspapers in Spain.

But—the reader will say—didn't you tell us you studied at Marburg? Yes, reader, it's true. I studied at Marburg, and at Leipzig and at Berlin. I studied deeply, orgiastically, and to the very limits of my being—for three years I was a pure Celtiberian flame burning, glittering with enthusiasm in German universities. I have argued Kant and Parmenides with Nicolai Hartmann, with Paul Scheffer, and with Heinz Heimsoeth, often late at night, on walks in snowy streets that ended at a railroad crossing while the monstrous Berlin Express went by, its red lights tinging the virgin snow blood red. Then for years and years afterward I was enthralled by German science until I almost drowned. In some of these sciences I am familiar with virtually everything done in Germany, both important and unimportant, and, since I have a fair memory, when I meet even a fifth-or sixth-rate scientist I can usually recall the title of one of his works tucked away years ago in the corner of some journal. All this is true, but it is also true that on the basis of my studies at Marburg, at Leipzig, and at Berlin I drew the conclusion that I *must*, for the time being—that is, for many years—write newspaper articles.

How? Why? It is a long story. But the very one I must tell in this preface for the German reader.

After the Counter Reformation Spain completely lost touch with Germany. On the other hand, beginning in 1700 the influence of French culture became progressively stronger—to the extent the Spanish soul allows this kind of invasion. My readers must always bear in mind that the man speaking to them belongs to a people characterized by its wars of independence in matters both territorial and intellectual. Spain in her hour of greatest abjectness, of greatest humility, of least faith in herself, has always refused with dignity to accept unreservedly the victor of the hour. The stricken Numantians refused to bow before the magnificence of Scipio, and, abandoned by his aristocracy, his king, and his state, the day-laborer of the harsh Castilian *mesa* spontaneously rebelled against Napoleon before anyone else dared do so. Paradoxically Spaniards have more often rallied to the vanquished than to the victors. Lucan's *Pharsalia* deploys its hexameters in homage to the unfortunate Pompey and not triumphant Caesar, and the *Quixote* is the epic of an eternally and essentially defeated knight.

Everyone knows this, but since the purpose of this preface is to make clear the meaning of the ideas printed in this book by sketching in the profile of the *man* who *says* them, it is necessary to remind the reader that an age-old experience of resistance, of independence flows in my veins. But a man of great experience means a mature man. *And the mature man is the one who has already seen the underside of things.* Keep this in mind. When I was twenty Spain was enormously influenced by French ideas and French ways. In addition there was a slight influence of certain English things. From Germany there was almost nothing at all. People talk about the famous Spanish *Krausismo*. But Krause's Spanish followers were what is called fine people but poor musicians. They exercised a considerable and noble influence on Spanish life, but all they knew of Germany was Krause. They had not even a clear notion of Kant or the German romantic philosophers who were Krause's contemporaries. And the reader will understand what an especially comic situation it must be to find oneself alone in a desert with the extraordinary Krause, Krause by himself, without those who came before or after, and without any of his contemporaries.

Therefore I owe a great deal to France and feel the French influence was very beneficial to Spain in its time. I say this as one experienced in resistance and independence. Why not say it! It is what I think. My intention is to reveal myself to German readers exactly as I am so there will be no risk of my books harming them. I must say at least *something* of what I think. This way the German public will be able to reject me *in time*, with the certainty that I will not complain. I am deeply, profoundly obliged for the attention it has shown me in recent years. *Nothing* could give me greater satisfaction. I am obliged, but I do not ask or beg for it. If, after getting to know me, a reader wishes to go on reading me, fine. If, on the other hand, he withdraws his esteem, that is fine too. I only know how to live with my accounts settled.

In point of fact I think every culture needs periodically to square off against another. And such an encounter requires prior knowledge of, as well as intimacy with, that other culture; in short, its influence. Furthermore, I feel this is one of the two basic facts about human history. The first is the appearance of autonomous cultures while the second is their cross-fertilization. And I consider it a scandal that the essential structure of a recurring historical event of such enormous import as the second has never been studied. What does it mean to say that one culture influences another? Above all, there is one exceptional, tremendous, almost monstrous, case, obvious to anyone with a modicum of historical sensibility. I refer of course to the fact that European culture has always been a symbiosis of two cultures: its own and Greco-Roman culture. In 1926, in presenting Ernst Howald's brief *Die Ethik des Altertums* to my fellow Spaniards—as I have done with so many German works—I wrote: "Greece is probably the most important secret of European history; that is, of the nations that sprang up from the ruins of Rome. Is it a glorious secret or a crippling one? This is the important question. Years ago I hinted at it. . . . Because we ought to ask ourselves whether European culture, so curiously dual in nature, so clearly derived from two antagonistic sources, is an integrated, healthy organism or a historical monster, a case of rampant parasitical growth. And if the second, which is the parasite and which the host plant?"

"The Spenglerian notion of historical pseudomorphosis is not applicable to the phenomenon of Europe. Because the manner of union of the Hellenic with our culture is not only a case grafting, of the mixing of both elements, but something much more surprising. For century after century, almost without interruption, whenever European culture needed an ideal, it always found it in the culture of Greece. Remember that what is innermost in a culture, most productive, the force that fashions it and drives everything else is a repertoire of longings, norms, of *desiderata*—in short, its ideal. And here we have a culture whose ideal, at least in part, is extraneous to it, in another culture in fact. This is the problem that I have not as yet seen clearly formulated and on which I hope considerable work will be done in the near future. . . . Because we carry so much of Greece within us, as the ideal inhabits

its enthusiasts, our relationship with Greek culture has always necessarily been bathed in religious or mystical hues and has never been the subject of a rigorous or impartial examination."

My expectations in this respect are still unfulfilled. Jaeger and his disciples seemed bent on inaugurating a new era in classical philology. Sure of itself, with all the technical, domestic problems solved, those purely instrumental ones that any science poses for itself, it seemed on the verge—at last!—of attacking the real problems, the ones life poses for us. There are always certain problems for which we are in vital need of fairly urgent solutions. Moreover, science has no mandate to concern itself only with its internal, domestic problems. Ultimately it exists to solve real problems, to be ready *at each moment* with a repertoire of answers for the most pressing problems of life. It must always be the *Summa*.[1] Because it has not been this, because it has tried to live for itself, science is having a very difficult time in the world today.

Why did Jaeger and his disciples not energetically attack this most urgent, thorny, and dramatic problem of the relationship between the Ancients and Europe? Because I respectfully submit, they adopted the eternal attitude of excessive piety. "There is too much piety with regard to the Greeks," I wrote in the same article. "There

1. Please understand me. My formulation would be as follows: (1) Science can only occupy itself with problems for which it has already assembled the necessary technical instruments. (2) But the problems with which it occupies itself in *this* way must above all be those that in each epoch most urgently confront man. *Later* it can turn to its domestic problems. In sum, science has a historical obligation to accept those problems a period places before it. Science must be organized according to vital needs. This will save science and be, *moreover*, a positive source of inspiration for it.

This obligation that the intellect has to attend to the problems of life must not, however, be confused with the *supposed* obligation to attend to the problems of the masses.

can be excessive piety about everything; about religion and about politics. Almost all political radicals, whether sincerely so or not, are excessively pious about democracy. In the same way there is an exaggerated piety as regards culture in general and the Hellenic in particular. And it is curious to notice that whenever this piety appears it has the same symptoms: a tendency to faint, to make extravagant gestures, to stare emptily, and an attitude of hopeless despair before all infidels deprived of grace. In the end, the only way to understand Greece is to put it from us, underline its foreignness and confess its enormous limitations."

But let us leave this subject. I was saying that at twenty I was totally immersed in the liquid element of French culture, and I went down so deep that I felt my feet touch bottom. I also felt that for the time being Spain could no longer derive nourishment from France. This made me turn to Germany, about which there was only the slightest knowledge in my country. The older generation had spent its life talking bout "German mistiness." What *was* pure mist was their information about Germany. I realized that what Spain had to do was absorb German culture, swallow it whole—as a new, magnificent source of sustenance. The reader must not, therefore, imagine that my trip to Germany was the journey of a devout pilgrim who goes to Rome to kiss the Holy Pontiff's feet. On the contrary, it was a rapid predatory flight, the arrow-like dive of a hungry falcon on something fleshy and alive that his round, bright eye has discovered in the countryside below. In my distant, impassioned youth I was in fact somewhat like the young hawk who nested in the ruins of a Spanish castle. Instead of a caged bird I felt like the fierce winged creature on a coat of arms; like the hawk I was voracious, haughty, warlike, and like him I worked with a quill. It was all clear then.

I was off to Germany to bring back German culture to a corner of the ruins and there devour it. Spain needed Germany. I felt my being—as you will see—so closely identified with my country that its needs were my appetites, my hungers.

But of course the beak with which one devours culture is called enthusiasm. If in my encounter with Germany I had not felt a sincere, profound, urgent enthusiasm for Germany's destiny—its longings, its fears, its ideas—I could not have done what I have been able to do. Because, reader, now it is a matter of record. The rapacious flight of that extravagant young bird with ruffled feathers has had its effect. In fifteen years of hard work things have changed with incredible historical speed. Today Spain knows German culture by heart. Knows it like the back of its own hand.

And another thing. Since this preface is a *unicum* in all my work, because I am going to use it to speak about myself—a thing that until now I have never done and that I have yet to do in Spain—I had better make good use of the opportunity and be cynical in the extreme. (It is characteristic of the cynic that with poverty and sincerity as a pretext, he rends his tunic so that others can see his flesh. Cynicism has always implied a bit of the exhibitionist.) Certain things that I have kept silent about for twenty years—even in private conversations—will be daringly revealed. The first is this: Germany does not know that I, and *virtually I alone*, have won for her, for her ideas and her ways, the enthusiasm of Spain. And something more besides. In the process I have imbued all South America with things German. In that continent across the ocean this has been freely admitted with fervor and solemnity.[2]

2. See *Die deutsche Philosophie in Argentinien*, a lecture given in Germany in 1930 by Coriolano Alberini, Dean of the Faculty of Philosophy and Letters at the University of Buenos Aires.

But Germany is unaware of this, and in Spain, where everyone knows, they have kept it to themselves. Even the Hispano-German Committee of Madrid, inactive for a long time like all such committees, feigns ignorance of it. This is why I am now forced in spite of myself to say plainly, with due cynicism, something I have kept quiet for twenty years.

But the German reader with whom I am engaged in dialogue will be thinking suspiciously: "Apparently this Mr. Ortega now wants us to pay our bill." Well, of course! There is no question about it! I have already said that I can only live with accounts settled. But remember: *first*, I am presenting a bill after, not before, German readers have spontaneously favored me with their attention, and *second*, I do it specifically by halting publication of my works in Germany on realizing, to my surprise, that their publication is going enormously well, and I present it so as to advise my readers to be careful that I do not turn out to be a dangerous writer for them. After nearly thirty years of "Germanism" it is only natural that I should have much to say to Germans, but what I will eventually say to them—my disagreement as well as my assent—can only be correctly understood if one knows, whether one wants to or not, all I have done to propagate German values, and knows as well that this will remain ir-remediably there, as a historical reality that runs its course and produces its own inexorable consequences in the mysterious landscape of the future. For a time I brought the Spanish-speaking world under the tutelage of Germany.

So I am presenting my bill to the German people, although not for collection here and now. Actually, I had already received payment, in the "world" I received from Germany. I was the debtor. But my accounts show the debt is paid in full, to the degree that a man can repay a nation. We are quits and now we can go on talking, equally free to pursue our own futures, which may well lie along separate paths.

3

How did my strictly scientific studies in Germany, undertaken above all in universities where, at the time, philosophy was highly technical, difficult, and esoteric, lead me to the conclusion that I must write newspaper articles?

I had spent a semester at Leipzig. There I had my first hand-to-hand struggle with the *Critique of Pure Reason*, which is so enormously difficult for the Latin mind; there . . . that is, sitting on a bench at the zoo, in front of the Canadian wapiti—at that time in the spring it was in full cry, threatening the heavens with its moist muzzle. Farther along, the elephant patiently—"genius is patience" —let a keeper file down the callus on its forehead. The elephant is a philosopher and presses his forehead against the bars of his cage, which is the best a creature can do. This is how he gets his callus. I too was getting a callus from continually butting my head against the bars of the *Critique of Pure Reason*—that spring—while at the bottom of the zoo the ducks chased each other, noisily giving themselves over to their indecent chores.

The next semester I was in Berlin, living on a small stipend from the Spanish government that I won as a prize. The *peseta* was then at a terrible low, and my living shrank to such an extent when I crossed the border that I could only afford to eat occasionally at Aschinger automats. On the other hand, there were the libraries where I could satisfy my hunger.

In 1908 I spent a whole year at Marburg; and in 1911 I returned with a wife. My first son was born there, in ripe May, on Saint German's day. So I named him Miguel

Germán. Miguel is a name for an earthbound German, who still lives on (and off) the land, that type of laborer who is the *humus* in which an entire nation flourishes. When a nation loses touch with the land, it loses all its strength, like Antaeus. Conversely, when a people have done all they were meant to in history and even their name is forgotten, their human dust remains in the laborer who goes on plowing up furrows as if nothing had happened. Miguel is the name of what there is before and after man. But Miguel was also the name of a very old friend of mine, a poor and profound Spaniard, who wandered the world with the saddest of hearts beneath the most courteous of smiles. But . . . perhaps you know him: this Miguel is Miguel de Cervantes.

Marburg was the fief of neo-Kantianism. One lived within neo-Kantian philosophy as within a beseiged fortress, always on the alert. Everyone outside was a mortal enemy: the Positivists, the psychologistic logicians, Fichte, Schelling, Hegel. So much were they considered antagonists that they were not even read. In Marburg one read only Kant and, once translated into neo-Kantian terms, Plato, Descartes, and Leibniz. Certainly these last were not insignificant figures, but it would be impossible to reduce the course of universal history to a smaller flow. The governor of the fortress, Cohen, was an enormously powerful intellect. German philosophy and philosophy everywhere owe him a great debt because he was the one who gave the rather violent shove that raised the level of philosophy. And this was decisive because philosophy more than anything else in life *is* its level. Cohen forced one to an intimate encounter with difficult philosophies and above all reawakened that will to create a system characteristic of true philosophical inspiration.

Nevertheless I must add three things. The first is that, properly speaking, philosophy was not *taught* at Marburg.

One had to know it already, to have been born knowing it. The neo-Kantian teachers were like the *druzes* of Lebanon, who do no proselytizing since according to them in order to be a *druze* one has to have been one from the beginning of time.

The second is that except for their extraordinarily fruitful desire to create a system the neo-Kantians did not lead young minds to the open questions that it was possible or interesting to work with. The only questions dealt with were those already assimilated to the canon. In general all neo-Kantian schools have been characterized by their thin repertoire of problems and preoccupations and their lack of curiosity. But this has to do with the third thing.

The third thing. . . . The third thing is something I hesitate to say at this point. It is much more serious. Perhaps later, when my pen is moving more easily, I'll take heart and reveal the secret.

Any life attitude that is called *neo*-anything, that is a return, a *zurück zu* . . . , is, of course, inauthentic. Human life would be the opposite of what it essentially is if from among the innumerable forms of life produced in the past, *that are already there,* we could select the one we prefer.

In truth, the human condition is staggering. The shape of man's life is not given or imposed on him as are those of the stars and the trees. Man has to choose his own being at each instant. He is *perforce* free. Yet his freedom of choice means that, while man feels an inner necessity to choose the best, what this best may be is not itself something that is his to decide. Among the many things that at any moment we can do or be, there is always one that appears to us what we *must* do, what we *must* be; that is, it appears necessary. This thing is *the best.* Our freedom to be this or that does not free us of the necessity itself.

On the contrary it involves us more deeply in necessity. Cosmic necessity consists in the inability of a star to deviate from its course. At the same time the trajectory is a "given" and the star is not obliged to make it up. The star's behavior—its being—is predetermined, and however enormous and bright, the star travels along like a child, asleep in the diamond cradle of its orbit.

The unfortunate human being, on the other hand, finds himself in an extremely difficult position. It is as though he were told: "If you really want to be, you have of necessity to adopt a very specific way of life. Now if you want you may choose not to adopt it and instead decide to be something other than what you must be. But then rest assured you will end by being nothing, for you can only be what you must be, your own authentic self." Human necessity is the awesome imperative of authenticity. Whoever freely chooses not to abide by it falsifies his life, he *unlives* it, becomes a suicide. As it turns out, then, we are invited to do what we are obligated to do. We are at liberty to recognize necessity. How courteous of our cruel destiny! We are told, very much as the severe county authorities in Calderón's *The Mayor of Zalamea* tell the noble, self-indulgent violator of maidens:

> With all due respect
> I'll have you hung, Praise God!

We can no longer be "Plutarchian men," "feudal lords," "courtiers of Versailles," nor "Jacobins." Or, rather, the terrible thing is that we can *try* to be them, but then our life is a masquerade. Every human life has to invent its own form; there is really no *zurück. The imperative of authenticity is the imperative to invent.* This is why man's primary faculty is fantasy, as Goethe once said, perhaps without realizing the profundity of his remark. Even what is called scientific thinking is nothing, *psycholog-*

ically, but a species of fantasy, the fantasy of the exact. Human life is, therefore, a poetic undertaking, the invention of that character that each person, each epoch has to be. Man is his own novelist. And when a nation's fantasy dries up, when it can no longer invent a program to live by, it is lost. I have already mentioned that the human condition is stupefying. And now life turns out to be, provisionally, a literary genre!

Yet it may be part of the tragic destiny of a generation not to find its own form of life. This is obvious! There are clearly generations that fulfill themselves and there are others that, in whole or in part, remain unfulfilled. Now then, one of the principal ingredients of a form of life is a repertory of ideas about the universe that is philosophy. The two generations of 1840 and 1855 were forced to live with a philosophy that was *not their own.* They borrowed neo-Kantian philosophy.

In some cases inauthenticity is a fault, but here it was inescapable. The *best* that those men could be was neo-Kantian. In the end transcendental idealism has been a profound catastrophe for philosophy. Hegel, one of the four or five greatest philosophers on our planet Earth, was possibly the least prudent. For the first time in this preface we come across the problem of the relationship between philosophy and prudence. Hegel's obvious lack of measure, his Nebuchadnezzarism, destroyed philosophy. The history of Hegelian philosophy is the history of Nebuchadnezzar.

The fields of Europe had been sown with salt as far as philosophy was concerned. With incredible swiftness the *technique* of thought that philosophy uses was forgotten. The result was a regression to infancy and intellectual prattle. This is why the generations of 1840 and 1855 had to go back to school, back to the classics. It became necessary to relearn the ABC's of philosophy.

Trendelenburg—three generations before—had already attached himself to Aristotle. Liebmann, Cohen, Windelband, and Riehl entered Kant's classroom. This was the primary meaning of neo-Kantian philosophy: a need for schooling on the part of a Europe that had regressed to philosophical childhood. This was also the reason for the curious intellectual style these men displayed; it consisted not in standing at ease in Kant's presence, but in placing themselves at his feet like insecure first-graders, *to see if they could understand him.* It was not so much a question of ascertaining the truth as it was one of understanding Kant.

Around 1870, then, there was no philosophy; far less did anyone pretend to have a philosophy of their *own.* So much was this so that there exists an especially moving case, and one that will interest all those students of the innermost secrets of Germany's, *and hence* Europe's, intellectual future.

As we will see later, I hold that a generation spans approximately fifteen years, but, for reasons I will give later, the exact placing of this span of years is a very difficult problem. However, allowing for the moment an approximate value to the idea of a generation, I would suggest that the two generations of neo-Kantians were born between 1840–1855 and 1855–1870. But before them comes a much more interesting generation in German philosophy. Cohen (1842), Riehl (1844), Windelband (1848), Natorp (1854) and Rickert (1863), will find the terrain less dangerous, the catastrophe less immanent. On the other hand, the generation preceding them was born to a period of utter desolation. They entered a world where only one *magister* and one survivor of high caliber remained. The latter was Lotze (1817), an extraordinarily perspicacious man with the keen scent of a pointer for new problems, yet a weak man, unable to withstand the triumph of antiphilosophy. For this reason his life was one of progress within a retreat. He was unable to inspire the younger men; quite the contrary. The *magister* was Trendelenburg (1802), a man who knew a good deal but whose *Logische Untersuchungen* show he lacked philosophical inspiration.

This generation, then, born around 1830, was probably the most unfortunate generation in the whole history of European philosophy. Who were its members? They are Sigwart (1830), Teichmüller (1832), Wundt (1832), Brentano (1838), and . . . no less a figure than Dilthey (1833). They are men of the Deluge, born in a shipwrecked era, philosophers *in partibus infidelium*. Yet in spite of everything two of these names heralded a brighter future. Actually, neither Sigwart, nor Brentano, nor Wundt, nor Teichmüller possessed what could be called a philosophy. They merely reached an accomodation with the situation, although Brentano managed several first-rate insights that were to prove extremely fertile. But what illustrates so movingly, in such a tragic-comic way, the extent to which no one dared *do* philosophy, is the fact that the only one with an absolutely first-class, authentic philosophy, the most important philosopher of the second half of the nineteenth century in Germany or anywhere—Dilthey—did not fully realize what he had. The case is an occasion for both laughter and tears. Dilthey spent his long and exemplary life in fear of himself, ashamed and in flight from his own shadow for he sensed that a whole philosophy, a magnificent ideological system, had lodged itself in his brain. This was why he never managed to articulate this body of thought that is nothing less than a marvel.

And the most interesting part of the story is that, with the exception of Wundt, these men were of a much higher caliber philosophically than the two succeeding

generations. In point of fact, not until Husserl's appearance do we find anyone like them. Their circumstances
simply worked against them.

The rest of Europe was entirely given over to Positivism, not itself a philosophy but something more and
something less than one: an intellectual set reached by
man in the course of his history, the result of a concentra-
tion of two hundred years of intellectual experience. At
any rate, this 1830 generation of Germans, defenseless in
their fear of having a philosophy, is probably the only
one since 1760 on which Anglo-French thought has had a
a strong and deep influence. Nevertheless, this is the most
authentically German generation to date, as the repertoire
of their concerns proves; for the fact is that in accord
with what I have just said, the Anglo-French influence
lay not in the imposition of specific ideas, but in forcing
these men to accept a mental ground, a basic disposition
—that of Empiricism. Today it is amusing to note that the
swan of Phenomenology was hatched from the hen's egg
that was Brentano's *Psychology from an Empirical Point
of View*, "*vom empirischen Standpunkt.*" The manner in
which Brentano and Dilthey were empiricists, especially
the latter, is still the way of the future of philosophy.

It is important to notice, as a clear example of what a
generation is, that these five men, so different in rank and
quality—one of them, Wundt, was especially hamfisted—
and so dissimilar in the ideological terrain traversed, had
nevertheless a common repertoire of intellectual concerns
that can be detailed as follows:

1. Unlike the following generation, they are rabidly anti-
   Kantian.
2. They tend to maintain that the whole exists before the
   parts.
3. That activity is before the thing.
4. That the whole and dynamism or activity are never-

theless something given, a fact and not a hypothesis.
This is why they are anti-Kantian. Thus for them the
categorical is "empirical," a fact.

5. That it is necessary to go beyond intellectualism.
6. They see the mental as the preferred reality upon
   which the world is to be constructed.
7. Therefore they will base all philosophy on psychology.
8. But on a psychology understood as a fundamental
   science and therefore viewed with an eye to its bene-
   fits for philosophy.·

That there should be room for a similarity of *interests*
with respect to these themes, within an area of such
breadth as that marked by the extremes of Dilthey and
Wundt, is the clearest possible illustration of the reality
of the concept "generation." These two fought *specifically* over these themes and felt themselves at opposite
poles. There was no way to settle the dispute between
Dilthey and Wundt on the question of the priority of the
whole and the parts. And in spite of this, Dilthey's basic
idea, and the "law of the *Schöpferische Synthese*" and
Wundt's apperception or "voluntarism" were simply two
different ways of grasping an idea that was entirely new
in the history of thought. Its newness lay above all in
that the totality, the synthesis, the *Zusammenhang,* was a
simple fact, while for Kant it was the very sign of what
was not a fact, but an act on the subject's part, something
subjective added to what was given as fact.

Any reader a little versed in philosophy will notice to
his surprise that current thought is based on these fundamental concerns; in other words, this is the generation
that is closest to us, this one rather than the two succeeding neo-Kantian generations. For it is unnecessary to point
out that our philosophy would have to be called psychology if placed in the perspective of 1870. Of course it is
only in Dilthey that the fundamental tendencies nourish-

ing us today realized their fullest and purest possibilities.

When the young men who between 1907 and 1911 learned their manual of philosophical arms in the fortress of Kantianism reached their twenty-sixth year—an age usually decisive in the career of a thinker—they were no longer neo-Kantians. We had not, however, completely wasted our time. We had studied Kant in depth, which is no small thing. More often than one would believe, even philosophers of a certain standing go through life dragging an insufficient knowledge of Kant behind them like a ball and chain. There is no making up for this lack because with Kant European thought swings a hundred and eighty degrees and takes its stand against the past in the form of a daring paradox. It is difficult for anyone well along in life to fill this lacuna in his education. In order to penetrate Kantian philosophy one needs the good will of those early years when good will is all one has.

Unfortunately, just as Kant made his momentous critical discovery, he became a dreadful writer; worse still, he became a dreadful expositor. This strange phenomenon should have been studied before now. Undoubtedly, the psychology of the father who has his only child too late, on the outer edge of old age, plays a part here. From the biographical point of view the child is an anachronism. At sixty it is hard to break a wild horse or to sketch in the typography of a newly discovered continent. Kant must have suffered from dizziness and a constant fear of becoming lost in the primeval jungle of his own invention. This was why he sought an illusory security in the strict artificiality of his book's architecture. The book's architecture, so carefully laid out, so geometrical, has almost nothing to do with the anatomy of his subject (his *Sache*) and tends to overshadow it instead. Imagine an exhausted explorer who reaches an unexpected coast and who, in order to set his mind at rest, pauses to draw an imaginary map of the new country before plunging into the interior. But all this will not explain the arteriosclerosis of diction and the lack of suppleness in technical nomenclature that afflict Kant's style during this critical period. It may even be that the "critical period" in Kant's own life, his physiological state, played a part. I have no time for Freud, whose work I felt it opportune to introduce in Spain for a number of reasons, but in which I have always had but a mild interest myself. So it has nothing to do with Freud's ideas when I state my feeling that, in general, literary style as such, to the extent that it is something in itself, separate from thinking, has as expressive function some relationship with one's virility. To put it in a somewhat exaggerated, rather grotesque way: the act of *writing*—I insist—*not* thinking, is a secondary sex characteristic linked in large measure to the evolution of an individual's sexuality. Every *blooded* writer knows that in the act of writing, *really* writing, his body participates with what are very like voluptuous sensations.[3] Who knows! Perhaps to a degree the writer writes for the same reason the peacock spreads his tail and the stag bellows in autumn.

Cohen's teaching in those years could not properly be called an exposition of neo-Kantian philosophy. Instead he brandished it like lightning, using it to destroy all its enemies, both real and imaginary. Because Cohen was a passionate man, philosophy became concentrated in him like electrical energy in a condensor, and the humdrum task of teaching amounted to giving off sparks and electrical charges. He was both a formidable writer and a formidable speaker. By the time I heard him lecture his eloquence was little more than pure pathos. But make no mistake, his was a pathos of the most exquisite variety.

3. What I call the "intrabody"; see "Vitalidad, alma, espíritu," in *El Espectador*, Vol. 5 (*O.C.*, Vol. II).

It was pure rhetoric; not *bad*, lymphatic, soft, or empty rhetoric. Just the opposite; for a German his phrases were abnormally brief, like the tensed sinew and muscle, the quick jab of the boxer. I felt each phrase like a blow on the back of my neck.

The curious thing about his sentences was that they did not usually convey the idea they were meant to express. No: they assumed that the listener already knew the idea, and expressed instead its emotional resonances and a readiness to pierce with a sword anyone who doubted their truth. He never said clearly what he meant by *"reiner Erkenntnis"* or by *"Urteil des Ursprungs,"* but rather transmitted to us all his enthusiasm for these ideas, his pathetic respect for their dignity and his disdain for those who refused to accept them. His word, whether written or spoken, had a warlike cast and, as is nearly always true of things warlike, although rather baroque, it was supremely elegant. From Cohen I learned to extract the feeling of drama that in fact inheres in every great intellectual problem or, better still, that every ideological problem *is*. The highest and most fruitful mission of the university professor is to trigger this potential drama and make his students feel that with each lecture they are the spectators of a tragedy.

Nicolai Hartmann is probably a few years older than I am, while Heinz Heimsoeth and I are the same age. The point is that in 1911 we were all near twenty-six, a decisive age in one's intellectual development, as I suggested above, but without giving any reasons. This is the time when a person—for the moment I speak of the philosopher—ceases being merely receptive as to major concerns and starts to show his originality. An examination of philosophers' biographies will show that with surprising frequency in their twenty-sixth year intellectual motifs that will later be seen as original contributions first show themselves. The essential or even the important thing is not that the specific ideas we later defend and develop occur to us then. Specific ideas are really nothing but the progeny of certain generic positions that are like the fertile wombs of these and other ideas. This is why at age twenty-six certain ideas do not *occur* to us, but rather we suddenly discover within ourselves, without knowing the origin, a certain disposition or desire that the truth possess a particular meaning and a certain composition. This disposition, which we are not aware of having formed but find within as a kind of intellectual terrain where we will have to live, is the human level that each generation *is* in the evolutionary process of human history. This is why it is not something the *occurs* to us but something we *are*.

What was this intellectual terrain in the case of our generation, the soil to which we would belong as the medieval serf belongs to his master's estate? In my opinion, what we *felt* or only vaguely sensed, what I am about to put into words, we neither thought then nor were capable of expressing.

The different varieties of neo-Kantian philosophy, as well as those close to it (and there were no others in force then) had a strange effect on us that we scarcely dared confess even to ourselves: they seemed . . . *forced*. The dots betray the indecision of my pen, which hesitates over the expression of a delicate point. It is delicate because rather serious and, *at the same time*, difficult to enunciate, easily misunderstood. With boldness it could be said in a minute: it would suffice to say that these philosophies seemed to us profound, serious, clever, full of truth, *and nevertheless without truthfulness*. These philosophies not only had a place for what was clearly true, but they also forced many things to seem true which were not, even for the philosophers who asserted them.

Our impression was, therefore, that thought could never move freely or at ease within these systems, if inhibited only by the strictures of honest proof. There was a great deal of orthopedics in their style of thinking. They took up the work of an author or a particular science—Descartes or Mathematics or Law—and obliged it to say *velis nolis* just what they had already decided it should say. The case of Natorp's treatment of Plato is incredible and exemplary. This Natorp, an excellent, simple, gentle man, with the soul of a turtledove and a Robinson Crusoe-like mane, was so cruel that he kept Plato locked in a dungeon for twelve or fourteen years, on bread and water, forcing him to undergo the worst tortures in order to make him confess that he, Plato, had said just what Natorp had said.

I speak of this in a frivolous way because I feel good humor is excellent for one's health, like sun, like the Alps, like a Japanese bath. But the point is a serious one, and I consider it a debt of loyalty to my German readers to bring it to their attention.

When speaking of philosophy our almost exclusive concern is with the problem of truth and error. We do not usually remember that there is another question as well: the truthfulness of philosophers. Here is the question about which it is difficult to speak without being misunderstood. And, in spite of this, it is a simple one: one has only to remember that truthfulness is nothing but a desire for truth, a longing to achieve certainty. So that whoever lacks truthfulness is not, without more ado, mendacious. It may simply be that such a person has other desires, other longings than those directed exclusively toward truth. The history of philosophy has not been examined except with respect to the degree of truth or error in its doctrines. This is natural. Truthfulness is such a constant element in the philosophical enterprise, it seems so essential to a philosopher's makeup, that we are loath to admit the existence of philosophers, of whole periods of philosophy, that were not truthful! If someone suggests the contrary, we reply that what he labels lack of truthfulness is simply the error a particular philosopher may have committed.

It would nevertheless be unfair to deny the interest of studying the history of philosophy so as to determine the greater or lesser degree of truthfulness that motivated philosophers and schools of philosophy. And just as such a study would make abundantly clear that this virtue has been the norm among philosophers, it would also raise to the status of important problems those cases where this virtue is absent. Then we would be moved to ask ourselves, with dramatic curiosity, with feeling, with a sense of urgency: How must they have been and what could have happened to those philosophers who possessed less than their share of this guild virtue of their craft?

I do not know what specifics a history of philosophy would uncover when written from this perspective, but when viewed from a good distance there is one fact that bulks surprisingly large in what is surely a vast panorama.

There have been quite a few splendidly prepared Germans who in the last twenty years have tried to make common cause with post-Kantian idealism. But the attitude they have adopted toward it and the work that has resulted from this attitude is, as far as I am concerned, a perfect example of what a nation should not be, of what can only have disastrous consequences for a nation. In the first place they have tried to make it synonymous with the essence of things German. This is a delicate point. Unquestionably there is something extraordinary in German idealism that actually does belong to the specific intellectual destiny of Germany. But it is extremely important that Germany separate this German "something" in Fichte, Schelling, and Hegel from what is not specifically German, but is instead a transitory, dying, and sinful moment, exclusively ascribable to a few groups, to several generations of philosophers. If we are to avoid what may be serious consequences for Germany, it is essential to isolate and leave chemically pure what is truly German in "German idealism"; in other words, the part of it in consonance with all that has happened in Germany since Arminius. But it is only possible to distill this "pure strain" in all its clarity if the other one is isolated as well, the part of this "idealism" that is not German but "Romantic idealism" instead. Then we would see that this whole prodigious creation poses a nearly unique problem in the history of human thought. "Romantic and quasi-Romantic idealism"—we may call it this to appease those who are so insistent on showing that Hegel was not *already* a Romantic—is probably the first moment in the thousand-year-old evolution of philosophy when philosophy became aware of itself, became self-conscious. For the first time it was clear that: (1) philosophy, whatever else it may be, is in one way or another, a system; (2) philosophy as a problem, as intent and as a mental set, has almost nothing to do with science; in short, it is not *one* of the sciences; (3) this mental set, philosophy, consists in a search for reality, not for abstractions, parts, or fragments of reality like the sciences. However, reality is no longer just the world, but something in which, in one way or another, man as such also intervenes and is.

This is why, with the post-Kantians, philosophy fully realizes its *intellectual form* for the first time. In this sense, if someone were to ask me to show just what philosophy is, there would be nothing else to point to in the history of mankind, and we would have to say: Fichte, Schelling, Hegel: that is philosophy!

At the same time, unless we want to go seriously and

irretrievably astray, it is absolutely necessary to examine another tremendous problem raised by the existence of this "idealism." Never before has the specifically philosophical genius more fully realized its potential, and yet this whole movement is unique, or nearly so, and this for one surprising, extraordinary reason: never before has a lack of truthfulness played such a large and important role in philosophy.

I find it surprising that this aspect of post-Kantian idealism has not been separated out and studied in depth, because those who have studied this brilliant work in the last thirty years know its shortcomings far better than I. They know that in spite of unusual constructive powers these men lacked intellectual scrupulousness to an equally unusual degree. There have been many mistaken philosophies in this world, but if there is any effluence from the whole history of philosophy it is that strange, frenetic nisus of philosophers for a thing called truth. There are only two periods when a desire for truth, when scrupulousness, gave way to a desire on the individual's part to achieve his ambition at any cost: with the Alexandrians and the post-Kantians. How did this happen? Because of their tremendous talent for philosophy and because they were so deeply imbued with the *intellectual form* of philosphy, the scandalous fact that they were not truthful is all the more obvious. A lack of precision in their terminology ought to have put us on guard. Every term in their work is full of secret trapdoors through which the most diverse meanings come and go, changing identities. They did not set out humbly to look for stray asses like Saul, but instead were intent on conquering the kingdom of a system whatever the cost. Today, now that we understand them perfectly again, we can also understand Schopenhauer's irritation with them, which only yesterday seemed mere insolence or resentment. They did whatever they felt like doing with concepts. As if by magic they changed anything into any other thing. Ideas of this kind can be camel or weasel with equal ease, like the cloud Hamlet pointed out to Polonius with the lightning rod of his finger. These men showed themselves to be at once philosophical geniuses and sleight-of-hand artists. Hegel is both Aristotle and Houdini. He bribed reality with his genius to get it to accept the yoke of his doctrine. Transcendental idealism ultimately meant direct action in philosophy.

This is why I must energetically oppose the unqualified identification of the Germanic with the post-Kantian. If I were German, one of the studies that would seem most urgent, most instructive, most "purifying" for the future of Germany, would bear this title: "Genius and Insolence in Transcendental Idealism." Other philosophers have made many more mistakes. Schelling and Hegel make perhaps fewer mistakes, but they more often lack truthfulness.

Patriotism, precisely since it lies in accepting the whole of a nation's tradition—as we accept, willingly or no, our whole personal past, even those acts for which we are now sorry—is under a constant obligation to distill the past and pass along only the best to the future. With respect to the future, patriotism has just the opposite function that it has with respect to the past.

This is why I must repeat my conviction that one of Germany's fundamental needs is to clarify this aspect of Romantic and quasi-Romantic idealism. For it is not enough to point out—the case is all too obvious—that the basic force behind their work was not strictly and exclusively the desire for truth, *aletheuein*. It is essential to discover wherein the positive meaning of their paraphilosophical inspiration lay. Schopenhauer did not see very clearly when he stuck his fabled splendid fox's snout into the affair. To the extent that he was still an eighteenth-century man, he failed to fathom these essentially historical problems. A giant himself, all covered with wrinkles and with acid in his veins, he was happy to wage war with three other giants, hurling whole mountain ridges of insults at them.

Nevertheless, he managed to sniff out a few of the elements that make up the problem. He surprised in these men a tendency to forget "the fact that one can feel an authentic and bitter seriousness" for philosophy, and in their work he missed "the deeply concerned spirit of a philosopher, whose whole grandiose seriousness consists in the search for a key to our enigmatic and uncertain existence." He also hoped philosophers like these could "learn as a habit of mind a true and fruitful seriousness, such that the problem of existence would capture the thinker and bestir his innermost being" (*Parerga*, II, 167, 186. Grisebach).

The solution to this enigma, which I have no intention of offering now, is perhaps to be found by recalling an elementary fact: that between 1790 and 1830 poetry and politics were dominant in Europe.

If we took the poetic and the political priorities as coordinate axes, perhaps it would be possible to solve this difficult problem of the post-Kantians' intentions.

At the same time I realize there are those who believe they have shown that truth does not exist, that what goes by that name is only a product of the individual or "collective" will. Nietzsche felt this way, if I remember correctly: "das Leben *will* Taüschung, es *lebt* von der Taüschung" (life requires fiction, lives on fiction). As for this opinion, I can respect it without sharing it. For I believe that only now have we finally managed to see clearly how truth is an essential ingredient in man's makeup. Although it seems incredible, until now it had remained unexplained why man must seek truth. Truth seemed an obsession, a luxurious, almost ornamental concern, a game or a pointless curiosity, perhaps an added convenience, or, as Aristotle thought, the expression of a *natural* tendency to exercise certain faculties. All these views presuppose that man can, after all, live *without* truth. His relation to truth was therefore extrinsic and fortuitous. This is why the Socratic expression that ὁ ἀνεξέταστος βίος οὐ βιοτὸς ανθρώπω—"man cannot sustain a life where there is no longing for truth" had always seemed mere words. But now we understand to what extent it is literally so. Life without truth is unlivable. Truth exists in such a way as to be man's reciprocal. Without man there is no truth, but by the same token without truth man is not man. He can be defined as the being who has an absolute need for truth and, conversely, the only thing that man needs absolutely, his only unconditional need, is truth. All other needs, even food, are necessary on condition that there also be truth, that is, that it make sense to live. Zoologically speaking, then, one would have to classify man as a *Wahrheitsfresser* (a veridivore) and not a carnivore.

The contrary opinion, that man can live on myths and without truth—in short, can live on falsehood—has, among other disadvantages, that of being a typical symptom that always appears in history whenever a rebellion of the masses and the consequent apotheosis of collectivization have occurred. The masses and collective states can, in fact, live without truth: they do not need it, nor are they capable of it. This leads one to suspect that masses and collectives are not man or are merely an unusual, deficient human mode. Who knows? . . .

In any case it was useful to raise here the grave question that post-Kantian idealism poses since, in spite of their hatred for Schelling and Hegel, the philosophers of

Marburg were unknowingly inspired by a laudable goal:
that of raising neo-Kantian philosophy to the level of
later idealism and, conversely, of containing speculative
idealism within the *naturalistic*, Newtonian frontiers of
Kant. The unfortunate thing about the closeness of their
purposes to those of the post-Kantians was that they became contaminated with the latter's lack of scrupulousness and excessive desire to be right.

This was the first reaction to neo-Kantian philosophy
that our young group of 1911 discovered in itself when,
instead of receiving ideas, its originality began to bestir
itself. For this awakening is what we spoke of earlier, and
a subject to which we must now return if we wish to
avoid losing ourselves in the seeming arabesque of this
preface.

I do not believe I betray what we found within when
I say that our common discovery consisted of three elements:

1. A commitment to truthfulness, to the strict measurement of ideas against what shows itself as reality,
without begging the question in any way. This has been
best exemplified in Hartmann, who proceeds with so
much circumspection that he stops when things begin
not to be clear and, turning to his reader, says: "This is
all I know on the subject."

2. The desire for a system, so very difficult to coordinate with the above commitment. For while the Romantics hungered for systems as for a ripe, round, sweet,
and juicy fruit, we saw it as the specific and difficult obligation of a philosopher. Seen in this way, a system
could not be the work of youth. And hence the tacit
decision that each one of us must have made to leave the
mature work for the proper time in life; this, as Aristotle
affirms with a disturbing excess of precision, is the age
of fifty-one.

3. Together with these formal attitudes, we also found deeded to us—unequivocally and without escape—the conviction that we must launch our ships and leave not just the province of Romantic idealism but the whole continent of idealism itself.

How strange is the human condition: To leave idealism is undoubtedly the most serious, the most radical thing a European can do today. By comparison everything else is trivial. In abandoning idealism one leaves not only a space, but a whole era: the "Modern Age." This is why in 1916 I called a short essay "Not Modern at All and Very Twentieth Century." But since, as I have said, there was no turning back—the inexorable slogan is that of Cromwell's men: *Vestigia nulla retrorsum*—where could we disembark? Those young men of 1911 set out for un unknown destination—"Ins unbekannte, niemals Betretene"—one that had never been reached before.

But did we have *concrete, positive* reason to know that idealism was no longer the truth? Doubtless we had many *negative* reasons, many objections to idealism. But that is not enough. Living truth is not governed by the laws of Scholastic argument. And no idea is entirely proven until we have grasped the clear, positive idea to be put in its place. Naturally, we had no such idea. But that is the strange part: we did have, unequivocal, extremely clear, an empty space for the new idea, its outline, just as the missing piece is a mosaic makes its presence felt by its absence.

Probably things have always happened this way in the course of history. Tomorrow's solid reality is first the foreshadowing of a desire; of a desire, naturally, that is itself not a matter of choice. Thus there would seem to be a *necessary* fantasy active in history that prefigures man's future, that outlines it as an existential project, as a program for life. Reality, then, is not merely the more or less accurate playing out of a plot that man as the dramatist of his own destiny has previously created. I think this idea will make possible extremely precise historical research of a new variety. At the same time it gives an immediate meaning to Shakespeare's idea that "we are such stuff as dreams are made on."

There was, then, no alternative but to pull for an imaginary coastline. A safe arrival was unlikely. Nevertheless, fortune had given us the prodigious instrument of phenomenology. That group of young men had never been, strictly speaking, neo-Kantians. Nor did they entirely place themselves in the hands of phenomenology. Our desire to be systematic kept us from doing so. Phenomenology, by its very consistency, is incapable of a systematic form or shape. Its inestimable value lies in the "delicate structure" of fleshy tissues it can add to the architecture of a system. This is why phenomenology was never a philosophy for us; instead it was . . . a stroke of good fortune.

But this shared awakening—around 1911—was also the signal for a separation. Age twenty-six—a few years earlier or later—marks the moment of essential decision-making for the individual. Until that date he belongs to a group and depends on a group. Adolescence is cohesive. During it, man cannot be, and does not know how to be, alone. He is ruled by what I have termed an "instinct for contemporaneity" and he lives in the mix of youth, in his "age class." But when that date in his life cycle arrives the individual sets out to meet his private destiny, which is at bottom a solitary one. Each one in history will accomplish the historical mission of his generation. Because ultimately each generation is precisely that: a specific mission, certain precise things that *must be done.*

4

In 1913 I wrote my first book, *Meditations on Quixote*.[4] It was a record of my own reaction to what I had received in Germany, which was, in the main, neo-Kantian philosophy and idealism. At the same time, 1913 is an important date in the evolution of German thought. It was then that phenomenology hove into view with the publication of the first *Jahrbuch der Phänomenologie*, where no less than such works as Husserl's *Ideas* and Scheler's *Ethics* appeared together.

Faced with this idealism, with all this philosophy of Culture and of Consciousness, my reaction was basic and unequivocal. It was this: "Life in society as well as all other forms of culture make their presence felt as members of the species of individual life." This is the fundamental reality. The rest is "abstract, generic, schematic," secondary and derivative as compared with each man's life, with life as immediacy. But this fundamental reality that is one's life consists not in "consciousness," in *Bewusstsein*, but in a fundamental unitary duality like Goethe's Gingko-biloba which was *one-two*. Our life, the life of each one of us, is a dynamic dialogue between "I and my circumstances." The world is first of all our circumstances and solely "through them do we communicate with the universe." Neo-Kantian philosophy, and in one way or another all philosophy then considered important, held on the contrary that man's *reality* was Culture.

But "culture [I said then] provides us with already purified objects that were once spontaneous, immediate life and that today, thanks to creative reflection, *seem* free from time and space, from corruption and caprice. They form a kind of zone of ideal, abstract life, floating

4. Published in early 1914.

above our personal existences, which are always hazardous and problematic. Individual life, the immediate, our circumstances, are different names for the same thing." Now then, it is imperative that we return all we term culture to its definitive reality, that is, to our individual lives. "All that is general, learned, everything achieved by culture, is nothing but the detour we must take in order to bring the immediate into focus." Culture, in spite of its solemn, hieratical mien, is nothing but the result of man's humble necessities. And vice versa: "every human need, if raised to a higher power, becomes a new realm of culture."

In short, we must give this famous culture roots—it pretends to be free of space and time, utopian—by accepting service in the space-time crew, assignment to a place and a date that is the fundamental reality, our actual life, and make this a principle in opposition to the abstract principles of culture. "We must search out in circumstances, just as they are, precisely what there is that is limiting about them, peculiar, a specific place in the immense perspective of the world. . . . In short: *the reabsorption of his circumstances is man's concrete destiny.*" Life's meaning then is for each to *accept* his inexorable circumstances and in accepting them make them his own creation. Man is the creature who is condemned to translate necessity into liberty.

"My natural access to the universe is by way of the Guadarrama passes or across the Ontígola plain. This sector of surrounding reality makes up the other half of my person: only by means of it can I become integrated and be fully myself." "I am I and my circumstances, and if I do not save them I cannot save myself. *Benefac loco illi quo natus es,* we read in the Bible." Life "is neither soul nor substance," but a precisely determined spacio-temporal "perspective," the opposite of all that is utopian, a *species temporis* as opposed to the *species aeternitatis.*

The rest of my writings, which have taken the form of an incessant battle against Utopian ideas, were already there in this, my first book.[5] Although, as I have often written, in an epoch like ours that encourages us to be *anti*-something, I have tried to be for and not against things, I have argued continuously against intellectualism, the root of idealism. This is why I have been and am the irreconcilable enemy of an idealism that, in locating space and time in the mind of man, has man existing outside of space and time.

I found myself in the beginning, then, with this basic twofold discovery: that one's own life is the fundamental reality and that life is circumstantial. Each of us exists as a castaway in his circumstances, and it is there, whether he wishes or not, that man must struggle to remain afloat.

But since life in its very "substance" is circumstantial, it is obvious that although we may think otherwise everything we do is done in view of our circumstances. This allows us to discover the true function of the intellect and of culture. Life confronted with circumstances is "uncertainty," "darkness," "shadows," "a problematic question," "preoccupation," "insecurity." By the same token, life needs "clarity," "security," "self-control." "Now then, this clarity, this complete control, is provided us by the concept. All the work of culture is *interpretation*—clarification, explanation, or exegesis—of life. Life is the eternal text, the burning bush beside the road where God cries out. Culture—art or science or politics—is the commentary, that mode of life in which life itself acquires polish and neatness through internal refraction. This is why the world of culture can never retain the problematic character typical of all that is

5. The preceding quotes are from the introduction to my *Meditations on Quixote* entitled "Reader" (*O.C.,* Vol I).

pure vitality, pure life. In order to control the unruly tor-
rent of life the sage meditates, the poet quakes, and the
political hero builds the bulwark of his will. . . . Man
has a mission of clarity on earth. This mission has not
been revealed to him by a God nor imposed on him from
without by anyone or anything. He carries it within
himself, *it is the very source of his constitution.*" [6] "The
vital concern that . . . first stirred in the breasts of the
Greeks and then spread to all the peoples of continental
Europe was a concern for certainty, for security,"—
τὸ ἀσφαλὲς της ὑπδέσεως [7]—Plato said; the certainty of the
hypothesis. Culture is the hypothesis we seek. "Culture is
not all of life, but only the moment of certainty, of stability, of clarity . . . , not a substitute for the spontaneity of life, but necessary in order to secure it; [8] and culture is above all "*aletheia,* which, as later with the word
apocalipsis, commonly meant discovery, revelation, or
more precisely, unveiling, the removal of a veil or covering." [9]

This was *my* own first reaction. It is clear that
twenty-one years ago I took a position not unlike what
has recently been discovered in Germany under the
name, wrong and arbitrary to my way of thinking, of
"philosophy of existence." How did I arrive there? This
is not the best time to explain in full. If the path to this
new intuition had been suggested to me by some personal influence, it would be easy to relate. It would be
enough to mention a name. But today everyone knows
that with outside help one could only arrive at the Idea
of Life as the basic reality by reading two thinkers:
Dilthey and Kierkegaard. Now then, neither I nor anyone in Germany—except *at the very most* his personal

6. *Ibid.,* 355.
7. *Phaedo,* 100d, 101d.
8. *O.C.,* I, 355–56.
9. *Ibid.,* 336.

disciples—suspected in 1913, or for a long time there-
after, that Dilthey had what could properly be called a
philosophy of human life. On the contrary, Dilthey
stood for the conviction that one could not have a philosophy. The best informed knew of Dilthey as a marvelous historian or a problematic psychologist. I was not
aware of his value in either guise. As for Kierkegaard I
have never been able to read him. Although I have enormous reader's jaws that gobble up the least promising
material without hesitation, I have been unable to ingest
a single one of his books. By the fifth page his style has
made me ill. To my mind one of the most attractive
things is a bear, but when I see a great Northern bear
who prefers to his own bear's dignity, to his bear
dharma, the pretense that he has quick, light, dancing
feet, it disgusts me. Kierkegaard may possess admirable
ideas, but his literary posturing has kept me from seeing
them. Moreover I suspect two things which I submit to
the judgment of German readers better versed in Kierkegaard than I; one is that he is another instance of that
eternal Christian who, instead of basing his Christianity
on something positive, ingenuous, generous, and fresh,
bases it precisely on the fact that reason is a limited,
tragic thing. That is to say, a species of Christianity that
is a mere objection pretending to be a positive quality
and to stand alone. But objections are only parasites. This
Christianity gets its sole nourishment from the presumed
failure of reason; it lives off a corpse. The gypsy's bear
turns out to be a hyena, and the fable about them becomes a bore. The fact that something is limited and
tragic in no way militates against its being an unquestion-
able reality, perhaps reality *itself*. Reason, above all "pure
reason," certainly tends to be insolent, but it was never
necrophagic. It appears in history when faith dies, but
instead of living off that death, it earns its keep by the

sweat of its brow. But this Christianity is constitutionally and permanently a failure of reason and the despair of man. It replaces the tragedy that is reality with a paradox, an intellectual game.

The other thing I suspect Kierkegaard of is the following: what he calls "existential thought," born of thought's despair, is very likely not thought at all, but instead an exasperated, arbitrary resolve, another kind of "direct action." This is why I very much doubt if any philosophy can be adequately termed "*philosophy* of existence."

Be that as it may, it is essential as Europeans adopt the point of view of life, of the Idea of Life, itself a fundamental advance over intellectualism, that they not let go of reason in the process, that there not happen what is told in this comic ballad:

> What with all the clouds of dust
> We lost sight of Don Beltrane.

In any case, I am especially concerned to point out that the beach where my ship came to rest was not any equivocal "existential thought," but what I myself would soon call "a philosophy of vital reason," in which reason is substantially and fundamentally vital but is no less reason for all that.

I did not reach the idea of life as the fundamental reality, as the pure event of man's struggle with his circumstances, by way of positive intimations from anyone. I was directed to it by the very problems that confronted philosophy. I repeat that this is not a good time to go into the whole question. It has little to do with the purpose of this preface. But, as a kind of cabalistic sign for those of my readers who concern themselves with philosophical method, I will say that my meditations took the following path:

There was always a scandalous ambiguity in idealism because while it held consciousness to be the fundamental reality, it still had never managed to analyze completely and with the required precision just what consciousness was. You will say that this was an absurd situation, but no one can deny that the history of thought is full of such absurdities. In the final years of the last century Husserl made the heroic decision to endow idealism with what it lacked: rigor, neatness. In grand style he submitted the ledger of idealistic bookkeeping to a careful auditing and imposed a norm of exactness on it. The fruitfulness of this undertaking was immense. Once again it was demonstrated—and despite the frequency we are always surprised—how the great advances in knowledge often come from close attention to small differences and not from important new intuitions. Keppler found the way to his momentous invention by obstinately insisting on the special importance of a minute discrepancy of eight minutes of arc which Tycho's rigorous calculations had ascribed to the orbit of Mars.

For the first time, then, phenomenology stated with precision the nature of consciousness and its ingredients. But when I undertook a serious study of phenomenology—in 1912—it seemed to me to have committed the same errors on a microscopic scale that the old Idealism had committed on a larger one.

The philosopher sets out in search of an exemplary, primary, and ultimately solid reality, to which he can refer and on which he can found all other realities. In pursuing this end he is suspicious of his own thought. The greatest tribute to a philosopher consists in something that is doubtless very amusing: he is a man who is by nature suspicious of himself. He knows he is naturally deceptive and so becomes his own detective. Thought is the subject *positing* something. In view of this the philosopher searches for a brief against all subjective positings. This brief must consist of something that he does not posit, but which instead *imposes itself on him,* of something therefore that posits itself, something "positive" or "given."

Now then, Husserl thought he had found this primary reality, this positive or given, in pure consciousness. Pure consciousness is an "I" that is aware of everything else. But understand one thing: this "I" does not *want,* it is only *aware* of wanting and of *what* is wanted; it does not feel, but only *sees* its feeling and the values felt; in short, it does not think in the sense of believing what it thinks, but is reduced to *noticing that* it thinks and *what* it thinks. This "I" is, then, a pure and impassive mirror; it is contemplative and nothing more. What it contemplates is not reality, but only a spectacle. The true reality is the contemplation itself; that is, the "I" that contemplates only when contemplating, the act of contemplation itself, and the spectacle contemplated *qua* spectacle. Just as King Midas turned everything he touched to gold, so the *absolute reality* that is "pure consciousness" makes *unreal* all that is given to it and changes it into pure object, into pure aspect. Pure consciousness, *"Bewusstsein von,"* makes a ghost of the world, transforms it into mere *meaning.* And since the consistency of *meaning* is exhausted when it is understood, this reduces reality to pure *intelligibility.*

This is clear enough, but now we must ask to what extent pure consciousness is really a positive value, a given, something "self-posited" that forces itself on us. The answer leaves no room for doubt: this pure consciousness, this pure *Erlebnis,* has to be *obtained* by a manipulation, by what the philosopher called a "phenomenological reduction." And this is a serious matter, as serious as what happens to the physicist when he wants to see inside an atom: when the scientist observes the atom he enters it, intervenes and modifies it. Instead of *finding* a reality he manufactures it. So with the phenomenologist. What he *really* finds is "primary consciousness," "unreflective" and "ingenuous," wherein man *believes* what he thinks, wants things in fact, and feels his aching tooth without any possible "reduction" of pain other than aspirin or an extraction. The *essence* of this "primary consciousness," then, is that nothing is only an object for it, but rather everything is reality. In it, being aware has no contemplative overtones, but is rather an encounter with things, with the world.

Now then, while an act of "primary consciousness" is taking place it is unaware of itself, it does not exist for itself. This means that this "primary consciousness" is not, in fact, consciousness. This concept is an incorrect name for what there *is* when I purely and simply live, that is, live without *subsequent* reflection. What exists then is myself and the things of various sorts around me—minerals, people, triangles, ideas; but there is not, in addition and together with all this, any "consciousness." For there to *be* consciousness I must break off living my experience in the present and, turning back my attention, recall what has just previously happened to me. This memory is nothing more than the retention of what *was* there before, that is, a real man who happened really to be surrounded by real things. But all this is now a memory and nothing more. In other words, now I find myself in a new situation: now there is a man, the same as before, myself, involved with something that is as much a thing as those previously mentioned, but of a new kind, that is, a memory. This memory recalls a past reality. This past reality is not, of course, real now. The present reality is its recall and this is what we may properly term "consciousness." Because now there *is* "consciousness" in the world, just as before there are minerals, people, and triangles. Naturally, however, this new situation which consists in my encounter with the *thing* "consciousness," and which is memory or, more generally, "reflection," is not itself consciousness, but is instead just as ingenuous, primary, and unreflective as the first one. I continue to be a real man who discovers before him, and therefore *in the world*, the reality "consciousness."

Once I have this entity, so to speak, in hand, I am free to do all sorts of things: I can observe it, analyze it, describe its consistency. But there is one thing I cannot do: it preserves a previous reality, and I cannot *now* change the reality that has already been, correct it or "suspend" it. That reality as such is now irrevocable. The only thing that can happen is that, for this or that reason, I come to hold the *opinion* that the prior reality was a hallucination or some other class of mistake. But this, of course, in no wise *undoes* the prior reality, does not make it unreal or suspend it. How can we now make something unreal that is no longer actual? How can we "suspend" the exercise of a reality that has already taken place, is no longer being performed, and of which there only remains the exercise of the *memory* that it was performed? That would be like suspending now, in the present, the beginning of the composition of the Edict of Nantes. The effect of this new opinion of mine is simply to really place me in a world where there are "mistaken" realities, that is, in a somewhat more complicated world than the previous one, but no less effective or real than it was. "Reflection"—I repeat—is just as ingenuous a real situation as the "primary" one and equally unreflecting with respect to itself. How could this new situation ever claim for itself the ability to bestow a greater degree of reality on what it encounters—a "consciousness"—than on what was encountered in the primary situation: minerals, people, and triangles?

The supposed "reflexive consciousness," designed to find that the *true and absolute reality* is consciousness and pure experience, is, on the contrary, *less* basic than the "primary consciousness," and for two reasons: (1) because it implies the existence of primary consciousness as its own "object" and (2) because, ultimately, it too is an ingenuous and unreflecting "primary consciousness." Every attempt to dislodge ingenuousness from the universe is in vain. Because, in a word, there truly *is* nothing other than sublime ingenuousness, that is to say, reality. Reality supports and *is* the world and man. In order for idealism to make sense an "act of consciousness" would have to be able to reflect on itself and not solely on *another* "act of consciousness."

The enormous advantage of phenomenology was to have worked out the question in such detail that it became possible to grasp the moment and place where idealism committed its crime of making reality disappear by transforming it into consciousness. It does indeed begin with an "act of primary and ingenuous consciousness." This is not of itself consciousness, however, but very reality, the toothache hurting, man in truth in the real world. The idealist presupposes reality, starts from it, but then from the vantage point of *another* reality he classifies the first as *mere consciousness*. But this is of course no more than an opinion *about* that unyielding reality, one that leaves it untouched and one which, by the same token, could it but be redirected against the situation of the opining idealist, would paradoxically destroy it. In *fact* the man convinced that what there *is* is pure ideality, "pure *Erlebnis*," is a real man who must deal with a world beyond himself, one made up, independently, of an enormous thing *called* "consciousness," or else of many smaller things *called* "noemas," "mean-ings," etc. And these are no more and no less things, inter-subjectivities, *things to be dealt with, willingly or not*, than the stones against which his body stumbles.

If the "consciousness" of which idealism spoke were really something, it would be precisely *weltsetzend* (that which posits the world), the immediate encounter with reality. This is why it is a self-contradictory concept, since for idealism consciousness means precisely the *un-reality* of the world it posits and encounters.

By suspending the executant powers of "conscious-ness," its *weltsetzung*, the reality of its "content," phe-nomenology destroys its fundamental character. "Con-sciousness" is precisely what cannot be suspended; it is irrevocable. This is why it is reality and *not* conscious-ness.

The term "consciousness" ought to be discarded. It was meant to stand for the positive, the given, that which posited itself and was not put there by thought, but it has turned out to mean just the opposite: it is merely a hypothesis, a fortuitous explanation, a construct of our divine fantasy. What there truly and authentically *is* is not "consciousness" and in it "ideas" of things, but rather a man existing in a landscape of things, in a set of cir-cumstances that also exists. Naturally, we cannot do without man's existence, for then things would disap-pear, but, equally, we need the existence of things, for without them man would disappear. But this insepara-bility of both elements is falsified if we interpret it uni-laterally as things depending on man for their existence—that would be "consciousness." What there in fact *is*, what *is* given, is my coexistence with things, that abso-lute event—a self *in* its circumstances. The world and I, set before each other, without any chance of fusion or separation, are like the Cabiri and Dioscuri, like all those divine pairs who according to the Greeks and Romans were always born and always died together, and to whom they gave the lovely name of *Dii consentes,* the "unanimous gods."

My coexistence with things does not consist in the fact that the paper on which I write and the chair I sit on are objects for me, but rather that before being objects, this paper is *for me* paper and this chair is *for me* a chair. Conversely, things would not be what they are if I were not what I am *for them,* that is, a person who needs to write, to sit down, etc. This coexistence does not mean, then, a static being-together of myself and the world, side by side in a neutral ontological realm; instead, this ontological realm—my existence or that of things—consists of the pure and mutual dynamism of an event. Things happen to me just as I happen to them, and neither has a primary reality other than that determined by this reciprocal event. The category of "absolute event" is the only one, from the viewpoint of traditional ontology, that can begin to characterize the strange and fundamental reality of our life. The old idea of Being which was first interpreted as substance and then activity—power and spirit—has to be further refined, rarefied even more, until it is reduced to pure event. Being is something that happens, a drama. Since all language is of static inspiration, it must be retranslated into the fluid meanings of pure event, and the whole dictionary changed into a calculus of tensions. The smallest static residue will reveal that we are no longer in reality, but have taken for reality what is only a precipitate of our interpretation, a mere idea of ours, an intellectualization.

What must be done is to excise from the word "Erleben" all its intellectualistic, "idealist" residue, all suggestion of mental immanence or consciousness, and leave only its awesome primary meaning according to which *something happens absolutely* to man; that is, he *really* exists and not only *thinks* he does, outside thought, in metaphysical exile from himself, delivered over to the essential foreignness of the Universe. Man is not a *res cogitans*, but a *res dramatica*. He does not exist because he thinks, but, on the contrary, thinks because he exists. The "modern" thinker must give himself a kick that will land him in the absolute outside, a feat Baron Münchhausen would envy. When a doctor asked Fontenelle what discomfort he felt at being ninety-nine years old, the acute old fumbler answered: "None, none, except . . . a little difficulty at just being." That is perhaps the best definition of fundamental reality, of what there truly is, of Life: being as difficulty.

Thus the idealist philosopher deceives himself when, in setting out after the given and the positive, after what he has *not* put there himself, he believes he has found it in a pure consciousness that is his own creation and a mere fiction. What remains as perfectly justified is his demand that thought—that great creator of fiction, that tireless *positor*—be subject to indictment by what is imposed on *it*, by what *posits itself*. This is the truly given. But this cannot be anything thought discovers once it has set out in search of a given, or the *result* of an *ad hoc* intellectual process meant to eliminate thought itself on a local level. Because the "primary reality" thus encountered will be merely the result of this whole enterprise and *its* positings, most of which will at best be negative ones. To imagine that by *suspending* the performance of an "ingenuous consciousness" its positing has been avoided, is to be doubly narrow-minded and to forget that there is a "tollendo ponens" mode. When I imagine I am removing the positing of my earlier "primary consciousness" all I am doing is positing a newly created reality: a chloroformed "suspended consciousness." Instead one must do the reverse: before setting out in search of what really exists, the fundamental reality, one should stop, and *not* move forward, not take *another* intellectual step, but instead realize that what truly exists is a man in search of simple reality, of what is given. Not something new, already there, that requires the maneuver of a "reduction" to be obtained or manufactured, but *what was already there* when the philosophical thinking began, that is, this selfsame philosophical impulse and all the reasons behind it, all that forces this man to be a philosopher; in short, *life* in its incoercible, insuperable spontaneity and ingenuousness.

What *is* "self-positing," what *is* imposed on a philosopher's thought, is all that stands behind him, gives him birth and, thus, what he leaves behind. The philosophical enterprise is both inseparable from what was there before it began and linked dialectically to it; it has its truth in a pre-philosophical realm. The most inveterate mistake has been to think that philosophy must always discover some new reality that only appears under philosophy's lens, when the character of reality as distinct from thought consists in its already being there beforehand, in its being prior to thought. Thus the great discovery thought must make is that it is essentially secondary, the result of a preexisting, not a "found," reality; a reality one may even want to avoid.

This was the road that led me to the Idea of Life as the fundamental reality. The essential steps—the anti-idealist interpretation of phenomenology, my escape from the prison that the concept "consciousness" had been, and the substitution of a simple coexistence of "subject" and "object," the metaphor of the *Dii consentes*, etc.—were set forth in my university lectures beginning in 1914, but especially in a lesson entitled "The three great metaphors" delivered in Buenos Aires in 1916 and published in excerpts in Argentinian newspapers and magazines.

Phenomenology's analysis of consciousness allowed it to correct Idealism and carry it to perfection, a perfection signaling the beginning of a decline, just as the summit beneath our feet is proof that the mountain is now behind us. But a further analytical attempt, this time on phenomenology's own concept of consciousness led me to discover a breach in it,

> e quindi uscimmo a riveder le stelle.

5

But on reaching this point my remaining readers— mountain-climbers more than likely—will return with renewed insistence to their question: Why, with so many ideas in your head, did you not take time to develop them adequately in concise, technically well-articulated books, instead of writing newspaper articles?

The appropriate time has come for a categorical answer: I avoided the exposition of those ideas so as not to betray the ideas themselves.

The idea that "a man's concrete destiny is the reabsorption of his circumstances" was not just an idea but a firm conviction. My ideas have never been "just ideas." Circumstances are also a perspective and as such they have a foreground and, behind that, a middle ground, and so on until a background is reached. Now then, Spain was and is the foreground of my circumstances, just as the background is perhaps . . . Mesopotamia. Moreover, the very concept of circumstances contains an explicit prejudice against Utopias and all *actio in distans*. Circumstances are, then, what is nearest, the hand the universe extends to each of us, the hand we must take hold of, clasp enthusiastically, if we mean to live an authentic life. This is the origin of the series of essays I wrote during those years in which in bringing the biological ideas of von Uexküll into philosophy, I fought against the idea that man inhabits *a* milieu. Because a *milieu* is no specific place; it is everywhere. And what seemed essential to me was man's non-ubiquity, his "servitude to a plot of ground." The *milieu*, once I was able to see it as my circumstances, became a landscape. Landscape, unlike the more abstract milieu, is a function of a specific man. The same corner of earth becomes as many landscapes as there are men or nations to traverse it.

In those essays I dealt repeatedly with every aspect of man and his landscape, individual man and, especially, a nation and its landscape. Among my publications there must be an old attempt—not, I think, translated into German—to explain the milieu's influence on man by inverting the usual relationship. It is not simply that the land makes man, but that man *elects* his land, that is, his landscape, that portion of the planet where he finds his ideal or life-project symbolically prefigured. People often forget that man is a nomadic animal, that he is always potentially migratory. This ability to leave, so basic in man that it finds its supreme expression in suicide, forces us to explain all settling-down by an appeal to free and personal reasons. Since man's choice of a terrain is personal and free, it is not always correct, satisfactory, or sincere, and there appear degrees of adequacy, from the people who live entirely at home on their native soil, not wanting or missing any other—like the Andalusians—[10] to those who are always ready to leave the place where they are. An intermediate example is the strange and permanent nisus toward the South that has always animated the German soul. Every nation carries within it a "prom-

10. See my "Theory of Andalusia."

ised land" and wanders, pilgrim-like, over the earth until they find it.

The precipitate of my years of study in Germany was a decision to accept my own Spanish destiny without reservation. It was not a comfortable destiny. Only a few years before, our war with the United States had deprived us of our last colonies, so that Spain was reduced to a fraction of her former self. In European history she had been the first imperial nation, both quantitatively and chronologically. She invented the modern idea of the state, the great national state, a thing completely different from the ancient states. Bolingbroke was the first historian to fully realize this, which is why he has the modern age begin with Ferdinand the Catholic. (Let my German readers not forget this. Let them not forget that there is a disquieting similarity between what Germany is doing and what we began to do toward the end of the fifteenth century: invention of the first *Weltpolitik*, "absolutism" or "statism," creation of the first state army, the techniques of authority, political militias to safeguard public order (the *Santa Hermandad*), the *Imperium*, playing down the individual, the expulsion of the Jews and Moors, a preoccupation with racial purity. As is known, the word *Rasse*, race, originated in Spain. When all is said and done, I know very little about most things, but I find I know quite enough in knowing a good deal about this. All I have to do is descend to the bedrock of Old Spaniard in me. During the modern age there was little Spain could teach Europe since the latter was in the throes of revolution and this revolutionary experience is the only one my country has never had. But of all today's Western nations Spain knows more than any other about the things Europe is beginning to do; because she was the first to invent their forms, the first to thoroughly implement them and . . . the first in experiencing their consequences. This is why I ask that the ancient voice of my race be listened to, ask it not for myself or my country, but moved by the almost extra-human altruism of a nation composed of men "who won everything and who lost everything," a nation that knew how to conquer and how to succumb, the two extreme positions that life allows).

As we have seen, life as the acceptance of one's circumstances implies that man cannot save himself unless he also saves his surroundings. My first book was the first in a series of studies on Spanish themes, to which I gave the collective title of *Salvations*. Nothing would have been easier, after winning a teaching chair at the age of twenty-five, than to model my career on that of the German *Gelehrte*. Nevertheless, I understood from the first that my destiny was to be just the opposite one. In a 1910 public lecture entitled "Social Pedagogy as Political Program," I said: "In other countries it may be right for the individual to deal with national problems in oblique abstractions: Frenchmen, Englishmen, Germans, live in an already established social environment. Their nations may not be perfect societies, but they are endowed with all the necessary functions and serviced by properly functioning organizations. Although I do not say he should, the German philosopher is able to ignore the destiny of the Fatherland. His life as a citizen is entirely organized without any effort on his part. His taxes will not be too heavy, municipal sanitation will guard his health, the university offers him an almost automatic means of broadening his knowledge, the nearest library provides him at no cost with whatever books he may need, he can travel at little expense, and when he has voted at election time he can go back to his study without worrying if his vote has been properly counted. What is there to keep the German from launching his ship on a sea of divine, eternal concerns, and spending the next twenty years thinking only of the infinite?

"With us the situation is very different: the Spaniard who tries to escape national concerns will find himself their daily prisoner ten times over, and eventually will realize that for anyone born between the Bidasoa River and Gibraltar Spain is the first, the whole, the peremptory problem."

I perhaps ought to say that there was another point I wanted to make but was afraid to mention, especially to an audience that would not have understood. In fact, I already felt *then* that in German science and in the existence of the German *Gelehrte* there was, in addition to splendid virtues, a serious error, a deviation from the supreme hygiene of life; just that lack of concern with the immediate surroundings, that tendency to live in the "Erewhon" of science, as if science itself were a country, a landscape where intellectual effort could put down roots. I have kept turning the subject over in my mind, and that is why a few years ago the *Neue Rundschau* promised an essay of mine with the title *Der deutsche "Gelehrte" und der französische "Ecrivain,"* which, of course, I never had the nerve to write. The reader must realize that I am a man who is as timid as he is audacious, who goes through life in an uncomfortable rhythm of starts and stops. Today I am distressed at not having published that essay. But the title gives a clear enough indication of the direction it would have taken. Now it is too late to say the same thing. Events have run their course in an all too obvious and painful fashion. To have said it then would have been to foretell the future, which is the only thing worth doing. (That is why one of the purposes of this preface is to reestablish the dates of my work, especially those concerned with political realities and collective spiritual states. For what has happened is that essays of mine that describe what is happening now have been published by German newspapers and magazines in the sincere belief that they had just been written when all were written some ten years ago.)

In fact I never doubted for a moment that I would lead a life diametrically opposed to that of the German *Gelehrte*. My personal destiny seemed then and still seems inseparable from that of my country.

But my country's destiny was, in its turn, an enigma, perhaps the most puzzling one in European history. Madame Förster-Nietzsche told a visiting Spaniard how once, when the conversation touched on the Spanish in her brother's presence, although he was already ill and distant-seeming, he raised the ruin of his distinguished head and with a voice from beyond the tomb, an echo-like voice, said: "The Spanish, the Spanish! . . . They wanted to be too much."

Certainly of all nations we are the one that has undergone the most radical change. We have come from wanting to be too much to wanting too much not to be at all. How is this possible? What does it mean? What can and ought to be the attitude toward the future of a nation that was once everything? When I lived with the young people of Germany I felt an affectionate yet melancholy stirring in my heart whenever I heard them say, with enormous conviction, that the Germans had not yet realized themselves, not yet forged a profile and a life-style of their own. They felt this "not yet realized ourselves," one of youth's privileges, as sharply as any pain, while I carried in me just the opposite feeling: the ache of "having already realized ourselves" and the awful question of whether it could be done again, the longing of Doctor Faustus.

This is why for many years all my work has been obsessively concerned with the problem of Spain. That is why in my first book you can read anguished cries like the following: "It is at least doubtful that there are any other Spanish books that are really profound. An additional reason why we should address our most urgent question to the *Quixote:* My God, what is Spain? On the face of the earth, amid the countless races, lost between a limitless yesterday and an endless tomorrow, beneath the immense, cosmic chill of blinking stars, what is this Spain, this spiritual promontory of Europe, this prow of the continental soul?

"Is there—tell me—a lucid word, a single radiant word to satisfy the honorable heart and the clear mind, a word to illumine the destiny of Spain?

"Woe to the race that does not halt at the crossroads before continuing on its way, that does not make a question of its own selfhood: that does not feel the heroic need to explain its destiny, to inundate its historic mission with light!

"The individual can never find his place in the universe except through his race, because he is submerged in it like a drop of water in an errant cloud." [11]

11. *O.C.,* I, 361.

2 Phenomenology and Theory of Knowledge

Sensation, Construction, and Intuition [1]

It seemed to me best on this occasion to take as the subject of my brief comments one that combines the attributes of wide application and sufficient concreteness.

There is no better subject for this purpose than the first problem of philosophy itself, the problem that is its threshold. Whatever the ultimate scope of the problems included under the heading of philosophy, there is an essential and primary one that characterizes this new scientific realm called the philosophical. This question is already posed by the very existence of any particular science. Every science is made up of a complex of judgments or propositions, that is, of intellectual, subjective acts that are characterized by their truth—in other words, by their supposed correspondence to a complex of objective situations.

This is to say that each science presupposes, assumes, that its own generic character as true knowledge is already secured. Put another way, every science either describes or explains, uses conclusion and analysis, when it does not specifically base itself on the laws and principles of other particular sciences. Nevertheless, it is not as essential that it do the latter as the former; every science is a theory or specific system of theories. Its particular subject matter dictates the amount of theory ap-

1. Paper delivered at the IV Congress of the Spanish Association for the Advancement of Science in 1913.

propriate to it, so that every science lays its own foundations to the extent that its theory is particularized, even while accepting and presupposing the constitutive condition of theory as theory *in genere*. In a sense every science first presupposes itself and then proceeds to found itself as geometry, optics, botany, or history.

Thus every science presupposes another whose subject is "theory" itself. Naturally, this science of theory is a specific science like any other. Its content alone would not distinguish it from other sciences. Nor would the generality of its subject matter, by virtue of which every other science presupposes it—since all science is theory—be enough to set the science of theory above those of space or movement as essentially superior or radically different. Sciences also presuppose the existence of grammar, without this being sufficient to raise grammar to a superior rank.

What is decisive is the peculiar behavior the subject matter "theory" imposes on the theory or science concerned with it.

Of course, if other sciences take the constituent elements of theory for granted, the science of theory cannot do so. While there is a separation or distinction between form and the content or subject matter in other sciences, here the form and the content are one and the same. Even while the science of theory is examining the nature of theory, it must proceed to its own foundation as a science. Nevertheless, this is not merely a question of simultaneity: for this science there is no distinction between examining its own theory and guaranteeing the method of that examination. One could say that if other sciences are transitive ones, the science of theory is the theory of theory, a reflexive science, or rather *the* reflexive science, the only one that can be so characterized. This is why it is set above the others.

In our case we can use another term that is the equivalent of "reflexiveness"; we can call philosophy or the part of philosophy that is the theory of theory, the presuppositionless science. However, it must be understood that a presuppositionless science cannot be a science entirely without supposition or hypothesis. Without risking loss of its scientific status it may contain suppositions that it later proves and even suppositions that it does not prove, provided it does not suppose as true something proven in another science or under auspices other than its own. In this way Descartes supposed that the physical sciences and even the purely theoretical sciences were possibly false. He did not have to prove that they were. He had no need to. Descartes did not suppose this as true. He did not suppose a truth as true; he supposed a truth as mere hypothesis.

Thus philosophy is born in a desperate situation. It has, one might say, to earn its living from the cradle on. Hence it goes to the root of things. It cannot depend on a capital or inheritance of certainties, on any acquired truths. What is usually called common sense is a residue of traditional evidence that provides a solid grounding for the uncertainties of the spirit in our daily lives. In this sense, as Kant pointed out, philosophy is the opposite of common sense, of evidence by tradition. Its task is precisely to breach common sense, to overwhelm it and erect philosophical sense in its place.

I am going to set out, in brief formulae, the three basic positions that today philosophy takes with respect to its most fundamental problem.

This is to find a cognitive function that by virtue of its own character, without any external guarantees and without mediation, will secure the status of truth for its contents. This exemplary function will then serve as a benchmark to which the derived knowledge can then be referred in each case, as to a criterion. We will term the generic correlative of this function, the genuine contents that we capture by means of it, being, truth, reality, objectivity.

Cognitive functions are functions of a subject, and we could set out all the imaginable forms they might take on a scale running from the least to the maximum activity of this subject. At the lower end of the scale we would place pure receptivity. Between subject and object there would be no intermediary. The object would not be represented by anything but would be present there itself as knowledge. Thus, if there were a purely receptive cognitive function and we could refer to what is received just as it is received, we would have solved our problem. When the object is there itself, there is no room for error. The place error might occupy is taken up by the object itself. And this very displacement of error is itself the definitive, analytical sign of the truth we are looking for.

In fact, this is the position of that extreme empiricism that is now expounded by Mach and Ziehen, for example. To simply and strictly know, that is, to coincide with being itself cannot consist in a process of systematization or reasoning, nor in judgment. All these functions require an activity, a spontaneity in the subject, in which it moves back from what is received and substitutes an ideal object for the primary one. Thus, a judgment is a retreat from the content of the subject and the content of the predicate, and the positing of a third content that is merely a relationship.

Nor does representation, understood as a memory or image, satisfy the conditions of unmediated knowing. Hume's distinction between idea and impression, based on the relative weakness of the former, seems increasingly inadequate. Representation contains an inner ref-

erence to a perception, the claim of an identity or adequation with something absent. Thus it coincides with a
judgment, a process of reasoning, etc., in that the object
thereby constructed is at least partially transcendent.[2]

Mach does not hesitate to distinguish between all the
complex functions we include as derived knowledge
under the names "representing" and "thinking," and sensation, the original form in which being is first available.

This is the first position that can be adopted by a
presuppositionless science, a science of theory: being is
sensation; knowing, its correlative act, is feeling.

As the product of an era this solution to the greatest
problem of our culture is—to say the least—rather suspect. Notice the attempt to locate the criterion, the very
essence of knowledge—"the supreme gift of man," as
Goethe wrote—precisely where man ceases to be an
agent and becomes mere passivity. Is not this lack of
confidence in man and this attempt to order and rectify
the specifically human by recourse to the subhuman
symptomatic of a whole cycle of European civilization?

Nevertheless, there would be no alternative but to
adopt this solution if, in fact, philosophy could discover
this passive function passively, or if the sensations that
conveyed pure objectivity offered themselves and did not
have to be arrived at by a logical, psychological, or physical analysis.

It is undeniable that in a strict sense we can only call
that subjective function knowledge in which being itself
is given us. This particular tenet of empiricism is un-
assailable. Knowledge cannot consist in the possession of
a "copy" or a "sign" of being. It is unnecessary to repeat
that to admit an intermediary term only compounds the
problem and imposes the burden of infinite regress on it.

2. See, for example, Th. Conrad: *Uber Wahrnehmung und
Vorstellung*, in *Münchener Philosophische Abhandlungen*, 1911.

Immediacy between the original act of cognition and being is the requirement on which all contemporary philosophy is in agreement, without there being the slightest sign of a break in their common postulate.

But Mach's empiricism betrays its own tenet. By viewing what he calls "elements," that is to say, the contents of pure sensation, as ultimate reality, he overlooks the fact that this act of pure feeling and its correlative, pure sensation, are limiting concepts, problems without solution, and not unambiguous realities that will serve as a starting point. We need the methodologies of physics and physiology and the whole reflective apparatus of introspection in order to isolate a pure sound. So that far from being *given*, pure sound and pure sensation are constructions of systematic science. We not only arrive at them through an application of science, but once we have them we find that they cannot be separated from our intervention, and that it is impossible to consider them a definitive possession apart from the process by which they were derived.

In short, extreme empiricism is self-contradictory. It holds that being is pure, sensational being because the act by which it is achieved is a simple given. But as it happens this given and its contents are, in turn, the result of an elaborate scientific conceptualization, that is, of active, constructive thought.

The fundamental contradiction of this point of view inescapably has equally fundamental consequences. If there is no real cognitive function in which being is conveyed to us without subjective distortion, if there is no way in which the object is *given* to the subject, we will either have to renounce or completely transform the meanings of the correlative terms "being" and "knowing."

More clearly formulated, we might say that being is that which knowing as such apprehends; but since there is no way for being itself to be known, we see how absurd it would be to look for a being that is distinct from knowing and transcends it.

In the ordinary view there is not a relationship of correlation but of subordination between being and knowing. It seems quite proper that the conditions of knowing should be derived from those of being, that the former should be adapted to the latter. It is not realized that being, too, is meaningless apart from its mutuality with knowing, and that for this reason it must also conform to certain conditions. It is a precise correlation; each term lives off the other without either being dominant. Obviously, because there is being, there is knowing. But the reverse is also true: because there is knowing, there is being. We said being was that which knowing as such apprehends. Notice that this proposition distributes the obligations equally.

In his concept of "elements" as constitutive of being, Mach posited something metaphysical in spite of himself —metaphysical in the bad sense of the word. Earlier we interpreted extreme empiricism as saying that reality is made up of the elements of light, sound, etc., because the cognitive function by which they are known, sensation, is completely passive. Certainly this thought can be found even in Mach's theory. But on the other hand this same writer expects us to see in these "elements" something prior to the distinction between subject and object. The "elements" are not, properly speaking, "sensations"; instead, once they exist we consider them to be in a dependent relationship to a particular complex of elements called the human body. So that first they were not our sensations, not contents of the psychophysical subject, but alien realities existing prior to any act of knowing. In short, transcendent reality, metaphysical being. From this it is clear that extreme empiricism's theory of knowledge begins by asserting a reality and then proceeds to derive knowing from it. Now then, this denies the *sine qua non* of the theory of knowledge: to work without presuppositions. Knowing cannot be derived from being for the simple reason that the positing of being is a cognitive act, a theoretical one that receives its truth-value from that of knowledge in general.

Noticing this perfect mutuality between being and knowing has brought us to empiricism's opposite number, to the Copernican revolution that Kant produced in logic. Let us go next to the upper end of the scale on which we set out the possible acts of cognition, from pure receptivity and passivity to pure activity.

If we cannot make contact with a transcendent being because no real act of pure receptivity is possible for the subject, neither can we admit some function of mixed passivity and activity in which something is *given*—for example, elementary perceptible contents—on which we build something new. No such compromise would save us from the contradictions of empiricism.

What solution remains? Only this radical one: nothing that could be called "being" *is* given in an act of cognition, if by given we understand that something alien to the act enters it, unchanged, something that nevertheless then becomes an ingredient, an element of cognition; thus, for example, empiricism holds sensations are the contents of our acts of knowing; contents that, however simple, are finally determinate, cognitive particles or cells that provide the noetic matter for subsequent, more complex determinations. Conversely, the Copernican solution will not admit as "determinate," as "being" something, whatever does not derive its determination from the purely spontaneous act of knowing.

This is the position of critical idealism, originating in Kant, that Cohen and Natorp hold today. Cohen has even said, abandoning the remains of empiricism still in Kant, that the raw material of knowledge is not the brute matter of sensations. So that the passive act of feeling is entirely excluded from the system of cognitive acts.

How is this possible?

It does, in fact, seem very unlikely that knowing happens by itself without receiving anything from outside. Common sense has great difficulty in relinquishing the idea of transcendent being, from which the subject receives its original objective data, once the two have entered into a real—psychophysical or metaphysical—relationship. This is the source of the concept "thing in itself" that Kant never managed to exclude from his system.

And yet this is not a real problem. It only seems so if we insist on viewing the problem of knowledge as a problem of fact, of cause and effect, occurring in space and time; this view automatically disqualifies logic as the science of theory.

If knowing depended on a factual relationship it would presuppose a subject and an object, one affecting the other through psychophysical causality; that is, the theory of knowledge would require the prior existence of particular theories of physics and psychophysiology; truth in general would depend on the truth in particular of biology.

Fortunately, contemporary thought is losing this contradictory prejudice. Knowledge is not a process but an ideal object. The psychological act of grasping a true proposition is quite different from the "meaning" of that proposition. Science is an object in the same sense that n dimensional space is, and of course the latter cannot be verified, and occupies no space at all.

Extreme empiricism's lack of confidence with respect to the higher noetic activities is replaced by extreme confidence in the case of idealism. Precisely because the subject is the agent and responsible for the act of knowing, pre- cisely because knowing is its creation, science can seri- ously put forth its essential claim to possess the truth. An unmediated union of knowing and being can only be achieved by making being immanent *ab-origine* to know- ing. Truth, reality, objectivity are the inner signs of knowing; they are the very matter of which knowledge is constituted.

In this way, having given up all recourse to transcen- dence, knowledge becomes a *construction* and being be- comes what is constructed. Sensations only acquire those characteristics of stability and transparency, of certain and unequivocal value that the term "being" implies, when they are transcribed according to a system of reference points chosen by thought.

Idealism constructs the whole scale of being from top to bottom, and the criterion for this construction is not any immediate evidence that is trans- or superrational, but is constructed in its turn as the primary instrument that makes possible all other particular constructs. So it becomes possible to renounce any material hypothesis, the presence of which challenges the very existence of logic itself.

In physics sensations are categorized by ascribing them to an ideal order of previously established places that we call a spatial-temporal order. Physical objects are not, as Mach affirms, complexes of sensations; it is precisely light as seen and sound as heard that physics tries to reduce to objective determinations. In general what is sensed is the very opposite of what is objective, its pure phenomenon, the objective thing as deformed by its individualization in a psychophysical subject. And the objectification of such phenomena consists in their referral to the single spatial and temporal order where they are converted into quantitative relationships with a "meaning"—in other words, where they exist.

As we see, scientific idealism continues the Platonic tradition as well as that which the latter sired in the Renaissance beginning with Descartes and Galileo. With Plato a concept of knowledge appears according to which knowing is "saving appearances." To save them, that is, to fix them in a series of connections. Knowledge begins with appearances and sets out to establish principles, that is to say, hypothetical situations from which it derives the appearances. Strictly speaking, the appearances do not exist, and the relationships that serve as principles do not exist when taken by themselves. What *is*, the truth, lies in the actual adequation between principle and problem, between hypothesis and appearances. The perceptible qualities only amount to a problem; on the other hand, the physicist's definition of movement does not of itself have truth-value. But when the perceptible qualities are derived as movement, when they are reborn, as it were, methodically transformed into movements, the hypothesis acquires generative power and changes what was formerly an X into a specific value. Then and only then does the hypothesis acquire the character of a principle or, as Plato said, "gives being" to the phenomena. This functionality between principle and problem, this mutual relatedness, constitutes truth. "No greater truth can or must you expect from a principle than that it answer for all the particular appearances," wrote Galileo in a letter to Bellarmino.

For idealism it makes no sense to search the mind—which is a particular reality—for a cognitive act. Knowing is not a psychic act but an ideal one. In order for an act of knowing to take place in an individual he must mobilize his entire psychological structure—he will have to feel, perceive, imagine, allow himself to be inundated by a sense of belief and conviction. Yet none of this is part of the act of knowledge itself, but only of its real production.

Now then, just as physics constructs the material world on the basis of methods or principles with which it organizes appearances, so logic responds to the problem of knowledge by reestablishing a final hypothesis in which the character of truth is embodied. Thus the concept of the Idea in Plato, and of Transcendental Unity of Apperception in Kant. Decisive in both conceptions is the requirement of unity. This is what gives the cognitive acts the character of necessity, of incomparable cohesion that we look for when we seek to identify being. The requirement of unity is the foundation of theory as such, the method of all methods. When a problem has received an interpretation that can exist in the unty of knowledge, we say the problem is solved and things *are* as the interpretation supposes. The unity of thought, then, is the criterion of both being and knowing. They are as different as activity and product, as the production of unity and the unity produced. "No other thing can we know nor should we expect of sensible things than that they be in consent with each other and with indubitable reasoning. It would be vain to seek *truth* or *reality* where these conditions are not met, nor must skeptics ask, nor dogmatists promise otherwise." Thus Leibniz with his term "consent" anticipated what Kant would call the "Transcendental Unity of Apperception" and also "unity of experience," and Cohen, more simply, "unity of thinking."

Two points remain obscure in this constructional notion of knowledge, two exceedingly important points. One is the necessity that the cognitive function start from a problem.[3] Of course, there is no alternative, but this necessity raises a difficult question for idealism. A problem is not simply nothing but something, and it contains a certain specificity, however simple and vague. Idealism can say—Plato already insisted on this—that problems derive from previous solutions to simpler problems. In fact there is no *first* problem, no "problem in itself." For each stage in the progressive series of solutions the previous solution is a problem. For philosophy the principles of the various sciences are problems, and for the sciences the same is true of the crude conceptualizations of pre-scientific thought, which, in turn, has continuously evolved throughout history. Perhaps it would make sense to say that history is the history of what was once a vital problem for man and has ceased to be so for us. I think, however, this difficulty can be satisfied by a theory of knowledge that views the act of cognition as pure construction.

The other difficulty is more serious. I am simply going to outline it in order to show how it leads into a third basic position in the science of theory, leaving the matter unresolved for various reasons, the most important being that this is the topic that now excites the most interest among philosophers—the question *sub judice*.

The problem is the following: Is this character of construction that we have described sufficient to define knowledge? Is knowledge solely and essentially the determination of phenomena according to hypothetical points of view? In short, even if we allow that theory is an activity, the generation of its objects, a determination in the literal sense of this word, is it only this? For, in the first place, the two terms whose "consent" makes up the

3. See N. Hartmann, *Systematische Methode,* 1912, pages 131ff.

act of cognition must somehow first be present to the subject in order for him to assert their coincidence. And by the same token this coincidence or consent is not a construction but merely something we notice, become aware of. So that, in its totality the cognitive act may well be construction of the object; but each step or moment in the process requires a simple intuition of the related terms. Thus, in a judgment, which is the instrument of construction, it is a question, according to idealism, of an identification worked on the subject by means of a predicate; for example, in the judgment a is the cause of b, a and b are the subject identified as causality. But the performance of this judgment requires the presence before me of a and b on the one hand and of causality on the other. This does not mean accepting the old and completely inadmissible concept of judgment which holds that subject and predicate are two concepts antedating the judgment or two representations in a psychological sense.[4] When I say "a round square is impossible" no one imagines the round square is a concept or even less a representation; and yet the round square was something as far as I was concerned, since I was able to make a judgment about its impossibility. For idealism the subject of a judgment is a pure problem, an X that only becomes something determinate in the sense of something truly determinate, thanks to the predication. But even allowing for this, something perfectly clear hovered before me as the judgment was made. That something may not have been a specific truth, and it may not even have been true, as the round square was not. But this would only mean that there is a deeper, prior level than that of constructive truth or its lack, than that of being or nonbeing. Notice that, as in the example given, there exist many "objects" —they must provisionally be so named—of which a

4. See Lask, *Die Lehre von Urteil*, 1912.

thorough knowledge obliges us to say that they do not exist.[5] How can such "objects" be present?

Yet what happens with impossible "objects" happens equally with all the rest. Anything can be the subject of a judgment, and as such—here idealism is correct—we agree that it is neither concept, knowledge, or truth. Yet it is no less present for all that, even when complete passivity is observed on our part. The truth that two and two equals four requires that we superimpose the meaning of this judgment on the two and the four *themselves,* which in a sense are there in person before our intuition, and that, in this superimposition, we also intuit their coincidence.

Thus intuition is a function that precedes even that in which we construct being or nonbeing. In consequence that passivity of which empiricism spoke reappears. But how changed it now is! For empiricism passivity was synonymous with sensation and the perceptible was the sole original content. But intuition touches all intellectual modes. With equal intuitive clarity we are presented with the content of a normal perception, irrational numbers, "the polygon with n sides," "Justice," and "Minkowsky's principle of relativity." [6]

The discussions provoked by this new principle of intuition of Husserl's are both varied and profound. Its very novelty means it is too soon to see its limits and its constitution. I am content to broach the theme with you

---

5. See Meinong, *Untersuchungen zur Gegenstandstheorie,* 1904, p. 9.

6. "Intuition" is neither perception nor representation, nor judgment, but a *sui generis* function that can be exercised equally on the contents of a perception and a judgment. The correlative of the perception is the "perceptible thing" located in space and enclosed in a specific portion of time. The correlative of the "intuition" is an *essence,* not subject to space, time, nor any predicate of reality.

so that it may serve as subject matter for discussions at our future meetings.

I will only add that it tends to assert against constructive idealism that everything is given us, not only sensations, and that knowledge is rather a recognition of the *essential* necessities that intuition presents us with. It would extend to all manner of objects what until now has been the exclusive privilege of mathematics and of the older formal logic.

Let us postpone until the near future the verification of whether or not it will be able to erect that presuppositionless theory of theories which Edmund Husserl has been working on in partial studies that are unmatched today for their precision and importance. Perhaps with the principle of intuition a new epoch in philosophy has begun.

On the Concept of Sensation [1]

SINCE OUR national output on strictly philosophical subjects has been so slight, this section of the *Revista de
libros* will devote more of its pages than other sections to
foreign books. In this way I hope by the year's end the
reader will be able to find here an index of the present
situation in philosophy, at least with respect to its most
important and decisive problems. The present juncture is
extremely interesting. We are witnessing a rebirth of
what Schopenhauer called man's "metaphysical hunger."
To people educated entirely in the nineteenth century,
which along with the tenth century was a time when
European philosophy was at its lowest ebb, this strong
young burgeon is probably incomprehensible. Nevertheless, whether they accept it or not, the phenomenon shows
clearly discernible characteristics.

I am postponing for the present the study of this phenomenon, which was the theme of some public lectures
I gave in the Ateneo in 1912, in order to give an account
of the first critical part of the doctoral thesis mentioned
below.[2]

Mr. Hoffmann is a disciple of Edmund Husserl, a
professor at Göttingen. This explains the principal thrust
of his work. The ever increasing influence of "phenomenology" on psychology has caused a very fundamental

1. A series of articles published in the *Revista de libros*, in
June, July, and September of 1913.

2. *Studies on the concept of sensation* (*Untersuchungen über
dem Empfindungsbergriff*) by Heinrich Hoffmann. Archiv für die
gesamte Psychologie, Vol. XXVI, books 1 and 2, 1913.

and salutory division of the latter into a descriptive and an explanatory part.

In present-day psychology, even in Wundt for example, two very different sciences coexist: one tries to describe and classify the phenomena of consciousness, the other to construct a causal model of the mental world. Unless the formal problem of their differentiation is faced, the difference between them will create havoc. The basic psychological concepts cannot be transferred from one discipline to the other, and when this is overlooked they lose all value and precision.

The author is especially concerned with one of these concepts: sensation. He examines current definitions of sensation as a mental *element,* such as those given by Ebbinghaus, Fr. Hillebrand, Wundt, etc.

The first would amount to what Hoffmann calls "pure sensation." According to Ebbinghaus sensations are those contents of consciousness "immediately produced in the mind by external stimuli without discernible intermediaries, above all without experiences, but merely due to the innate structure of the physical organs on the one hand, and to the mind's own spontaneous way of reacting to nerve impulses on the other." In this definition what is considered sensation is something that according to the definition itself could never be found in the real consciousness of an adult. For there all content is merged with experience (memories, images, etc.). At best, then, such "pure" sensations could exist only in a newborn child's consciousness. With this in mind it becomes clear that here we have to do with a hypothesis analogous to the one about atoms in physics. "Pure sensation" is an ideal object, a product of methodical reflection with the purpose of rendering possible an explanation of the *genesis* of mental phenomena. Far from being found in real consciousness, it is an open problem, an *x* to be determined asymptotically. According to Hoffmann this concept is necessary for genetic psychology but is meaningless for descriptive psychology. (It is nevertheless curious that the most extreme proponent of a purely descriptive psychology—Natorp—should support a similar concept of sensation in his *Introduction to Psychology* of 1888. I hope the new edition, whose second volume has yet to appear, will somehow offer a correction.)

As for the Wundtian concept of sensation, it may be summed up according to Hoffmann as "a purely intensive and qualitative, simple state, separable from the various sense perceptions by analysis." Here sensation turns out to be an element of real consciousness, which because of its elementary nature never appears separately and on its own, yet is to be found in the primitive immediacy of consciousness by simple description. It is not, like the newborn child's sensations, a content of consciousness distinguished by the opposite characteristics of those possessed by our adult consciousness, but instead is discovered by the reduction of this mature consciousness to a final, unanalyzable remainder. According to Wundt, sensation is what is simple, what cannot be further analyzed. (That is, leaving aside the affective side of consciousness.) If Ebbinghaus' conception is generic, constructive, and hypothetical, Wundt's satisfies the criterion of descriptive psychology by limiting itself to the immanence of the spontaneously given.

Up to this point Hoffmann's study offers nothing new. Nonetheless, his rationale for submitting Wundt's thought to careful scrutiny is worth reading. In addition to certain difficulties inherent in the conception of psychic elements held by the famous psychologist—which, as I will show elsewhere, are greater than Hoffmann realizes—it is obvious that beneath its surface clarity Wundt's exposition suffers from a serious lack of precision.

Hoffmann proceeds with extreme empiricism: he does not try to form a generic concept of sensation. His claim is that to formulate one it would be necessary to study each class of sense phenomena separately. Thus he finds that both Wundt's method of definition and his definition itself are satisfactory for what is heard but not for what is seen. In the first case we actually do discover "relatively independent" contents as Wundt suggests: sound that is simple, but only relatively so since it is still characterized by intensity and quality. Of course both these components of simple sound are entirely abstract or, to put it another way, the mode of their differentiation belongs to an abstractive *toto coelo* principle different from that by which we move analytically from a chord to its discrete sounds.

The relative ease in abstracting the "simple" elements from complex sounds is not duplicated in the case of visual complexes. If we ignore what Wundt calls "colorless light sensations," in what does the simplicity of a color consist? The criterion that it cannot be reduced to even simpler elements is not as valid here as it was in the parallel realm of acoustics. There is talk of four basic colors. Are these the actual visual sensations? Wundt holds that in immediate consciousness—about which we can only speak descriptively—the basic colors are no different from the colors in between. Orange is just as simple as red or yellow. Wundt departs—more than Hoffmann seems to notice—from his own criterion of simplicity and replaces it with one of "saturation." Simple colors are *"gesaettigten Farben."* And, nevertheless, as we move from red to yellow we perceive the latter in a succession of *combinations* until it stands alone: so that the colors between red and yellow appear as complex. This is why psychologists in general accept a view that contradicts Wundt, according to which only red, yellow, green and blue are simple colors. This shows that the subject is still in doubt.

How much this is so would be clearer if there were time to mention the splendid work of Jeansch and Katz, both of whom have heavily influenced Hoffmann, even though he only mentions the latter.

And finally, while aware that the concept "simple sensation" is useful for psychology, Hoffmann refuses to accept it, because "it is a goal rather than a starting point for investigation, and consequently the theory of sensation must begin with sense formations that are more complex and susceptible to precise determinations."

At this point Hoffmann ends his critique and begins his phenomenological description of visual perception, covering a scale from greatest to least complexity only to arrive at a curious term, "sensible inwardness"—"*das sinnliche Erlebnis*"—and there break off without saying explicitly if the "sensation" he seeks lies in this direction.

The doctoral thesis we refer to is a welcome product of a certain innovative movement that has its center in Göttingen. And it would be useful to expound and discuss its method and conclusions, taking as the subject of an extended commentary a whole group of recent works conceived in the same or nearly the same spirit. We therefore set aside Hoffmann's primary subject, which may be called a phenomenological concept of sensation.

2

When we perceive something and its perception is really what interests us, we *live* completely in the act of perception. Put another way, in the moment of an interesting perception other acts may make up our consciousness—for example, wanting, feeling, and even thinking—in addition to the act of perception, but the axis of our attention passes only through the latter and it becomes the center of our mental life. This preference of our attention for a specific act in each moment is what we express by saying that we live completely in the act.

But when we judge, when we say, for example, "this is white," we perform a complex act whose elements are quite dissimilar. It contains a pure act of predication in which we affirm the "whiteness" of "this." But this act of predication is impossible without two other acts in which we are presented with the "whiteness" and the "this" to which we refer. In the example we are using, "this" means a present visual object, and something, therefore, that can only appear to us through an act of perception; "whiteness," on the other hand, can appear in an act of perception, but also in a mere act of imagination, perhaps an act of fantasy.[3] Perception, imagination, and fantasy are three classes of acts that can be reduced to one if we confront them with the predicative act. Compared with it they have in common the function of simply and immediately presenting objects. Predication is not an act of presentation, but it necessarily presupposes such acts. A judgment then, is a second order act *grounded* on presentative, or first order, acts. Or, better still, a judgment is a structure of acts in which there is a *grounded* act and basic or *grounding* acts.

Now then, this unity of different order acts entails a functional relationship among them which consists, provisionally, in that while I attend to the higher order act—in this case, predication—while I live in it and am aware of it only, I do not attend to, am not aware of, the other concomitant acts. And in spite of this there is no doubt that I perform them, no doubt that at that moment they constitute my consciousness, as much as the higher order act does. By the same token, when the sight

3. I refer to the subject, so current nowadays, of color fantasies on the part of those blind from birth.

of something irritates me I am aware of the object as the object of my irritation, not just as an object of sight.

Every judgment, we said, is grounded in presentative acts. But are these presentative acts independent? Are they not grounded in other even simpler acts? The question, thus posed, tends to distribute the entire fauna of our acts of consciousness along a scale where each order requires the previous one as a ground. On the one hand, there would be a class of situations for consciousness in which a duality of elements is essential: definitive acts or those to which we primarily attend, and peripheral acts (peripheral with respect to our axis of attention) in which the former are grounded. On the other hand, we face the particularly acute problem of whether there is another type of situation for consciousness in which it consists of a single act. In the previous type the interrelational functioning of central and peripheral acts seemed essential. We could say that consciousness consists of a dynamics between a zone of attention and one of inattention, as if in order to be aware of something it were necessary to have other things of which we are unaware.

To resolve this difficulty and to arrive at the essence of these simplest acts which ground the complex edifice of our integral consciousness, it is necessary, then, to subject the most important presentative act—perception—to a detailed analysis.

3

But first a few words about the method of this analysis. We have purposely postponed until now an answer to the question: What is phenomenology? What we have just been saying is an example of phenomenology, and now it will be easier to formulate a definition.

The proposition "Every judgment is a second order

act grounded in presentative acts" has the validity of a law. What is the basis for its validity? In order to derive this law there was no need to examine many real acts of judging, but only concentrate on a single one. What we have is not, then, an inductive or empirical law that only holds for the facts already observed or, at least, for the realm of experiences limited by conditions of fact, that is, limited to the existence of a specific species, man. No; the proposition is valid for any creature capable of judging. It does not express a factual connection, as is the case of the law of gravity. It does not prescribe the conditions of space and time (the factual ones) to which the judgment is subject, but instead proclaims an absolute necessity: that a judgment is impossible without an act of presentation, no matter who judges, whether it be man or God.

Nor is it a deductive law; we did not begin with the concept of a judgment, of judgment in general, in order to find there, analytically, as Kant would say, a need to be grounded in other acts. In deduction the single case does not give knowledge. Against the inductive approach we said it was unnecessary to examine many cases of judging, and accumulate statistics, etc., while against deductive reasoning we said that we needed a real, current act of judgment because in it and in it alone could such a law be discovered. . . . We do not extract the law from the concept of judgment, but from the judgment itself, from any judgment performed in fact or imagination.

This is not so strange as it might appear at first glance. One look at something colored is enough to establish this law: "There is no color without extension over which the color extends." Now, this law could not possibly be derived from the concepts "color" and "extension" by themselves. On the other hand, the validity of this law does not depend on the fact of what I see now—the way the law of gravity depends on the physical fact of the stars' positions in space. Therefore it is true not because *I* cannot *in fact* separate color from extension, that is, it does not depend on my factual constitution, on what I can or cannot do. It is not even a question of whether I can or cannot do something: the law states that it is color that is unable to free itself from extension.

Induction and deduction are indirect methods of deriving true propositions. This is clearly expressed in their names; with these methods truth is inferred or deduced but never seen. A proposition arrived at by either method bases its certainty in the last analysis on the formal laws that logic lays down for induction or deduction in general. So that although a deductive proposition may refer to material objects—optical ones, for example—its truth derives from the assimilation of what is seen to purely logical concepts. Just as in John Stuart Mill all inductive truths depend on the truth of the axiom (?) that proclaims uniformity of movement in Nature, although this axiom is really a whimsical invention of John Stuart Mill or, at most, a reasonable expectation. Thus assertions about a physical object do not derive their cognitive validity from what the object is itself, but from a combination of what we are given of the object and the general axiom about induction. And if this axiom were to shift slightly, it would collapse all our assertions about concrete objects.

The same thing happens with deduction. Here too the truth of an objective proposition is obtained by abandoning the object in question for other propositions that are felt to have already been proven true.

This is not to say that induction and deduction are inadequate scientific methods. It simply means that they

cannot aspire to the rank of primary methods for ob-
taining truth.

The proposition "Now I am looking at a table covered with books and papers" does not derive its truth
from anything that is not part of the objective situation
referred to. The proposition simply puts into words an
evident, actual, uninferred, objective situation. The possibility of hallucination does not jeopardize its truth, because it does not speak of an object existing independently and apart from my vision, but about what I see
as I see it.

Now then, the proposition presupposes that I can be
aware of individual objective states: this capacity is called
perception, imagination . . . or, more generally, experience or *individual intuition*.[4] By this I mean I become
aware of an individual object, that is, an object here before me in a moment of time and a point in space. The
table I mentioned is an individual object because it is an
object before me now and only now, here and only here.

In every individual object, then, there are two elements: one, what the object *is,* the table, with its shape
and its color, etc.; and the other, its existential moment,
here and now. This second element is what makes an
object a fact. As time passes and spatial relations change,
fact ravishes the object it encloses like a shell, and this
is why we say that only absolutely transitory things are
immediately present to us, only continual change. But
this is an error: in every individual intuition we can
set aside this element which individualizes and makes
the object a fact, so that only the object remains, freed
from its temporal and spatial coordinates, unchanging,
eternal.

My act of seeing the table extends in time; the physi-

4. Ed. Husserl, *Ideen zu einer reinen Phänomenologie,* 1913.
p. 10ff.

cal table that I see decays, but the object "table I just saw" is incapable of decay or of change. My memory of it may be vague and confused, but the table I saw, as seen by me, is a pure and immutable object. It is not an individual object but *an essence*. The individual intuition, the so-called experience, can always be transformed into an essential intuition.

Let us see how:

There is a "natural way" of realizing acts of consciousness, whatever they may be. This natural way is characterized by the executant value of those acts. Thus the "natural attitude" [5] in an act of perception consists in believing that something is really there before us, and that it belongs to a realm of things we believe to be real and which we call the "world." The natural attitude for the judgment "*A* is *B*" lies in believing absolutely that there is an *A* that is *B*. When we love, our consciousness lives unreservedly in that love. And we characterized such acts when our consciousness lives them in the spontaneous and natural attitude by speaking of their executant power.

Now, let us suppose that once our consciousness has effected an act of perception in the ordinary way, *in good faith*, that it then reflects upon itself and, instead of *living* the contemplation of the sense object, contemplates its own perception. Then the perception with all its executant completion, all its assent to there being something real before it, is suspended, as we might say; its completion is no longer effected since now it has only a *phenomenal* completion. Notice that this reflecting of consciousness on its acts (1) does not disturb them, for the perception is just as it was before, except—as Husserl so graphically says—it is now placed in parentheses; and (2) does not presume to explain but

5. Husserl, *ibid.*, p. 48ff.

only to observe them, just as perception makes no pretense of explaining the object, but merely takes note of it with complete passivity.

Now then, all acts of consciousness and all the objects of those acts can be placed in parentheses. The entire "natural" world, and science as a system of judgments executed in a "natural way," can be reduced to *phenomena*. But here "phenomena" does not mean, as in Kant, anything that suggests something else substantial behind it. Here phenomena means simply the virtual character that everything acquires when we suspend its natural executive value and view it contemplatively and descriptively, without awarding it a definitive character.

This pure description is phenomenology.

4

Phenomenology is a pure description of essences, just as mathematics is. The subject matter whose essences it describes is everything that makes up consciousness.[6]

Such a definition brings phenomenology perilously close to psychology, and in fact Husserl's early investigations, before he arrives at this clear formula, were subject to a psychological interpretation. Husserl himself, in his *Logical Investigations*—in 1900—spoke ambiguously of phenomenology as a "descriptive psychology." Here was a new area of problems that even the discoverer himself could not take in at a single glance.

Nevertheless, it is obvious that the new science is not psychology, if by psychology we understand, as is customary, an empirical, descriptive science or a metaphysical one: It differs from the common approach of psychology because it is exclusively concerned with *essences* and not existences. In general, psychology deals

6. Husserl, *ibid.*, p. 139.

with the *facts* of the human psyche, just as astronomy deals with the facts of celestial bodies; the existence of human consciousness is a constitutional precondition without which psychology would be meaningless. On the other hand, this same precondition is only necessary so that there can be phenomenologists; it has no direct effect on the constitution of phenomenology itself. Naturally, there is a place for a special phenomenology of human consciousness; this is perhaps what interests us most of all—but how is it possible without a general phenomenology?

Although, if duly considered, what has just been said is more than enough to establish an unequivocal distance between phenomenology and psychology, there is another point to be made that will further serve to underscore the difference. Human consciousness—the subject of psychology—is, to put it simply, a rather strange object, even stranger than that "salutary reason," that "salutary understanding," about which happier epochs than ours were wont to speak. Because the addition of "human" undoubtedly betrays a prudent attempt at limitation, one lacking if we speak of "consciousness" *simpliciter.* We are thus confronted with two heterogeneous elements that aspire to combine into a single thing: human consciousness.

In fact, by consciousness we understand that final court of appeal in which in one way or another the being of objects is constituted. If, in speaking of "human consciousness" we are concerned, as are the positivists, with restricting the qualities of *being* and *nonbeing* in order to completely relativize them, we at least require that the limiting object in which we enclose the rest, so as to control them, not be itself a relative *being* with limiting qualities. In short, the most extreme relativism and anthropologism require an unlimited and absolute meaning for the term "consciousness"—a proof of the inherent contradiction of both views—within which the object "human consciousness" can be constituted as one more object along with the rest.

When Descartes conjectured that all our predications about things are erroneous, when he had, therefore, put all transcendental objectivity, all affirmation or negation of the reality of things in parentheses, he noted that in so doing he had not exhausted the realm of being; for if all our transcendental propositions have been placed in doubt, as mere *cogitationes* they continue to have a validity, an absolute being. In the *cogitatione*, in consciousness, all objects enjoy an absolute status. Real being, transcendental being, may be other than I think it is; but what *I think is* just as I think it is; its being lies solely and precisely in its being thought. There are two sides to what is real: the part that *appears* to consciousness, that manifests itself, and, in addition, the part that does not. Thus a solid body is in essence a duality; because of its three dimensions it cannot become manifest, *appear*, except as a series of partial *cogitationes* (which in this case we will call perceptions), first of one side, then of another, etc. But since it has depth it has also an *inside* that can only come to light through an infinite number of serialized perceptions; so that what it is as a total reality can never manifest itself, become phenomenon, become consciousness. And this is why physics can never be a pure and exact science.

On the other hand, a triangle is purely and simply what we think it is, what it is as consciousness.

This plane of primary objectivity in which everything is no more than what it is as *appearance* (*fainomenon*) is consciousness, not as a temporal and spatial fact, not as the reality of a biological or psychophysical function ascribed to a certain species, but as "consciousness of."

By way of ending this brief account of what we understand Husserl's phenomenology to be, here is an example. Metallic glint is that peculiar, visible luminosity we perceive as surrounding this silver object. A physicist examines the special invisible combinations that produce this phenomenon. A psychologist examines the psycho-physiological mechanism by which we arrive at this perception. Thus the physicist looks beyond the phenomenon of "metallic glint" to the composition of the material thing from which the glint emanates. The psychologist investigates the genesis of the glint in a real human mind. Both begin with the *phenomenon* but abandon it for real objects, that is, for scientific ones, products of a process of rational construction. But before this it would in fact have been better to have reached agreement on what the "metallic glint" itself is—or rather, on what types of colors, and in what arrangement these must appear in order for the metallic glint to be seen. In short, one must decide the *essence* of what I see just as it is when and only when I see it. Does this seem a self-evident and unnecessary goal? Make the attempt and you will see that it is an extremely difficult task. In all likelihood no one has ever given a satisfactory description of such an ordinary thing. But once we possess it we will have a definition of "consciousness of" metallic glint; a definition that holds equally for the human, the subhuman, and the superhuman realms. Every subject for whom the metallic glint exists, whether earthly or divine, will perceive it in the same essential way.

As we see, phenomenology can boast an enviable ancestry that lends it historical dignity without depriving it of originality. All classic idealism—Plato, Descartes, Leibniz, Kant—takes its departure from phenomenology's first principle. Before they are real or unreal, objects are objects, that is, immediate presences for consciousness. The novel thing about phenomenology is that it makes a scientific method out of its unwillingness to abandon this plane of the *lived*, the immediate and the visible as such. The error to avoid lies in trying to place pure consciousness within a partial class of objects like reality if it is the level of the *Erlebnisse*,[7] of primary and all-encompassing objectivity. Reality is "consciousness of" reality; so that consciousness can hardly be, in its turn, a reality. It is all very well for psychology to conceive of "human consciousness" as a reality that appeared in our world on a specific day and at a definite point

7. Husserl, *ibid.*, p. 139. I take this occasion to ask help on a lexical question of all those interested in Spanish philosophy if, as I believe, Spanish philosophy means only that philosophy explained in terms that are truly meaningful to Spaniards. The case to which I refer is all the more curious since it is a problem that has now captured the attention of the whole of German philosophy, and yet it is a problem, nevertheless, for which only fifty years ago German thinkers would have had to discover or else invent a new word. This word, "Erlebnis," was introduced, I believe, by Dilthey. After musing on it for many years in the hope of finding an existing word in our language to translate it, I have had to give up and turn to a neologism. Here is how it was arrived at: in expressions like "living life," "living events," the verb "to live" assumes a curious meaning. Without losing its deponent value it takes on a transitive form signaling the kind of immediate relationship into which the subject can enter with certain objects. Now then: what shall we call each instance of this relationship? I can find no other word but "vivencia." Everything that arrives at my "I" with enough presence to become part of it, is a "vivencia." Just as the physical body is a unity of atoms, so the "I" or body *conscio* is a unity of "vivencias." Like any new word, I know this one sounds odd. Nevertheless, it already exists in compounds such as *convivencia* (living together), *pervivencia* (survival), and so forth, and follows similar forms. Thus: from *existir* (to exist), *existencia* (existence), from *sentir* (to feel), *sentencia*. Of course the dictionary of the Academy does not contain these composite forms, which makes me wonder if they are not somewhat exotic. I therefore request philologists to take an interest in this decision of mine. Until another, better term is found, I will continue to use "vivencia" as the equivalent of "Erlebnis."

in space; but it must never be forgotten that it is not because it is "consciousness" but because it is "human" that it is a proper object for clinical study. Mechanics is a piece of pure consciousness whose truth or falsehood, together with its axioms, reasons, etc., has no temporal or spatial coordinates. How could it become an object of study for a clinical psychology? It is not and could not be; that would be like studying the pull of gravity on the rules of chess. But psychology can study how and why the ideal body of mechanics, the "consciousness of" mechanics, came to inhabit the body of an Englishman on a specific date. The subject of explanatory psychology, then, is not consciousness itself but how the contents of consciousness enter and leave a body or, if you prefer, a soul, a reality.

What is reserved to phenomenology is the literally boundless field of the *Erlebnisse.*

Let us now interrupt this brief report and return to Hoffmann's study.

5

The "degrees of visual sensitivity" are Hoffmann's main subject. His purpose is to distinguish the distinct forms of "consciousness of" a *thing*—in the usual sense—that make up a real perception. Or, put another way, what elements must be present to a subject before he sees something. The elements sought are not to be taken genetically but descriptively.

In fact, this larger purpose is abandoned for a more modest one. Hoffmann only pursues what one of the senses—sight—contributes to perception. His main purpose was to arrive at a clear conceptualization of the simplest perceptual element: sensation. We will soon see how far he is from realizing even this latter task.

To begin with, Hoffmann distinguishes between what

physicists call a "thing" and what is commonly meant by the word. A "thing" for the physicist is a complex of atoms, by definition imperceptible, to which certain equally imperceptible qualities are imputed; it is thus something that can not be seen, a rational entity, an abstraction. Physics attributes the so-called "secondary qualities" not to things but to their mechanical influence on our sense organs. On the other hand, "when we speak of things in everyday life we understand by them something corporeal that fills a real, not a geometrical space, that is in this or that position with respect to other things, that has color inside and out, and to which we attribute a specific degree of hardness, smoothness, or roughness, etc." Physics starts with these properties and, rejecting some while adding others, arrives at what Hoffmann calls the "atomic thing" as opposed to the "perceptible thing."

This "perceptible thing" is the content of a whole perception: a thing of a certain shape, with an inside and an outside, that we see existing before us now in space.

Here a new analytic distinction becomes necessary. Undoubtedly, in a fully realized act of perception we *see* things as bodies, that is, as *full*, not composed merely of surfaces. Yet all our senses ever show us are surfaces. So perception would already appear to be a synthesis of two different kinds of consciousness: one which gives us the thing's surface, and one which alludes to an inside. Hoffmann skirts the problem of how what is called the interior of a thing comes to our attention, restricting himself to the question of the surface properties of things. Since, at the same time, he only refers to visual perception, we may designate its correlate the "real visual thing." [8]

8. Every act of consciousness is reference to an object by means of the "intentionality" of the act. The correlate of the act

Take, as an example, any distant object beyond our reach. A cube placed several meters away always shows three sides in such a way as to never coincide with the shape we believe the real cube has. With any change in viewpoint or distance on our part the form, size, color, etc. of the cube changes, and nevertheless, we see it as still the same cube. The "real visual thing" consists, then, in a series of views of a thing that assures us we are looking at the selfsame object. And it is essential to what we understand by a real thing that this series of views be literally infinite. We cannot exhaust the points of view from which a thing may be seen. So that according to Hoffmann it is a limiting concept, what Kant would call an *idea*.

If, from what we recognize as present in perception, we subtract what really is not, there remains a series of real views that can never adequately give us the real thing, but which gives us something we will always take for the real thing. If I walk completely around a chair, a continuous series of images unfolds before my eyes, finally becoming a closed circle. Is it correct to call this a real thing? Of course not; that completed series represents only a fraction of the views I might have of the object. If the grain, the roughness, etc. of the wood is not apparent from the distance I kept in my first turn around the chair, these properties will appear when I draw closer. The new distance will allow me to complete a new closed series. By what right can I term one of these series or any other the real one?

These things, obtained through a completed series of views, are, then, something that seems to approximate

---

is not the object—for example, the sun I talk about—but that "immanent object," that meaning by means of which I think or refer to the sun. The correlate of the act of perception is what is perceived, not the transcendent object. This distinction, although difficult to grasp, cannot be explained here.

what we call reality but is not it. Using Hering's terminology, Hoffmann calls them "visual things" (*Sehding*) as opposed to real ones. In contrast to the latter, "visual things" are really present to view.

Whatever in the "real thing" is not a "visible thing" belongs to what we can call the ideal factor in perception.

Here is an example: Size, a certain size, is a property we regularly attribute to all things. I do not mean the metric size—proper to the "atomic thing"—but the apparent size we customarily ascribe to an object. Now then, the trees at the end of an esplanade have a smaller "visual size" than the nearest ones. A cup is ten times larger a meter away than it is at several more. In addition, the "visual size" varies with the individual. Hoffman says there are those for whom the full moon at the zenith is the size of a quarter and others who see it as two feet across. I have found especially curious differences in this respect.

Then what is the size of the "real thing"? From the different sizes we select *one* and make it *the* size. Hoffmann calls this the "natural size." Each thing has a "zone of distance" within which it seems most itself. The size it has within this zone of distance is elevated to a norm. There is no way of arriving at a general law about what this zone will be, except that it will fall between the nearest distance from which the entire object and its parts can be seen, and the greatest distance at which the object still retains the size it had at the smallest distance.

A curious complication arises here. A part of a house—a brick, for example—is not seen in its "natural size" when I see the entire house in *its* "natural size." In especially large objects the natural size is not a simple sum of the natural sizes of its parts. Of course, it may be possible to tally up the parts in their natural sizes and thus obtain a size for the whole that will be the sum total. But this would be a constructed sum, not the visual size of the object in our example of the house.

Hoffmann goes on to make interesting observations about the kind of dependency between the variations in visual size and the variations of the retinal images. In my opinion these remarks are not germane to the phenom-enological problem that moved me to cite this section of Hoffmann's monograph. I only reproduce his conclu-sions here so as to be able to refer to them later when I speak of sensation. As a thing moves farther from the eye the natural size of the visual thing diminishes less than the metric size of its retinal images. Thus, instead of a strict correspondence there is a relative independence between the physiological base and the image.

It is even possible that without a change in size of the retinal image the visual size may be different. Place a pen thirty or forty centimeters away and it will be its natural size. Keep the same distance, put a window behind it, and adjust your vision to the window frame. Then the pen will appear much larger.

We must now look at other, even more important, phenomenological constituents of the "visual thing" such as shape and color.[9]

9. [The essay ended here.]

Consciousness, the Object and Its Three Distances (Class Notes)[1]

THE CENTAUR AND THE CHIMERA, fantastic creatures, are more than nothing; they are something, and something perfectly discrete and susceptible to clear description. It would be ingenuousness disguised as extreme wisdom if someone were to come forward with the objection that the Centaur and the Chimera are, *in reality*, no more than images or representations of ours, that the Centaur is really not a Centaur but a subjective image and the Chimera is really nothing but a representation. What advantage accrues to our heeding this prudent observation? By images and representations we simply mean modes, states, or situations of consciousness in which a thing or quasi-thing is present to us in a certain way. In other words, the image—a psychic reality—is an image *of* something; in, with, or through it we imagine something, and that imagined or represented something is not an image in its turn, not a psychic reality. While I speak now there are as many images or psychic realities as there are listeners in the hall—and, what is more, each person has an image of one and the same thing: the Centaur. Each listener will imagine it in his own way just as each one sees this selfsame lecture hall from the place he occupies. So that

1. The class for which these notes were prepared was part of a course given in the fall of 1915 and January, February, and March of this year [1916] at the Centro de Estudios Historicos [Madrid].

with this bit of wisdom behind us we end up where we were: The Centaur is not a real being—what is real about him is the real image or particle of our mind in which we imagine him; he is an imagined being, a fantastic being, a being of fantasy. But the effect of this, far from exiling him from the realm of being, is to situate him more firmly in it, to mark out a sector there for him to inhabit. The rose, which is real, is so because it occupies a real space and point in time; but the reality of this space, this time, and this rose does not mean or signify for the present anything more than the immediate sensual character appropriate to them. The rose is real because it is a visible and tangible being, because it is a perceivable being, a being of perception. In the same way the Centaur is a fantastic being, one of fantasy. Thus perception and fantasy are merely different ways in which being comes to our attention. We do not see sounds or hear colors, but this is no grounds for questioning their reality; so perception and fantasy merely qualify or classify beings, things.

In saving the Centaur's life, so to speak, we have also gained something for ourselves; we have purified our ordinary, everyday, common sense notion of being. Reality, things, and perceivable beings are synonymous in common parlance. And at the same time they constitute the whole of being. Now, having taken notice of an unreal and imperceptible being, we will have to correct the usual terminology. We will let the word "thing" continue to mean what it has meant—whatever can be perceived. But we need to find a term that will convey what it is that real and unreal beings have in common. And what they have in common is simply the following: they are the targets of consciousness, what it is conscious of in its different modes, what we aim at when we see, imagine, conceive, judge, love, or feel.

Apparently I can never manage—we are working with appearances only at this point—to discover my consciousness except when it is not only occupied with something of its own—a perception, an image, a judgment, a willing, or a feeling—but occupied moreover with something other than itself. All sight is sight of something; every image, an image of something; in every judgment I judge *x* and, what is more, judge something about *x;* my wanting or not wanting is a wanting or not wanting something; my feeling of pleasure or displeasure flows over me, but as though proceeding from something that is pleasant or unpleasant. One could say, then, that wherever and however what we call consicousness exists, it is always composed of two elements: the attitude or act of a subject and a something at which that act aims. The act itself may take many forms: it may be one we call seeing, or fantasizing, or else plain understanding; it may be loving—and it may be being moved or affected. In every case we have different ways of being concerned with some thing, a thing with the essential property of appearing distinct from the acts of the subject. There is nothing so different from my seeing as what I see; from my hearing, as what I hear; from my understanding, as what I understand. What the lover loves is that woman, perhaps a dark-skinned creature from Seville—but his love for her, the *act* of feeling love has no skin at all, nor is it from the south of Spain. The lover may even turn out to be Basque. And again: when I speak of something as unintelligible or unthinkable no one would suggest that what I refer to with these words in any way resembles my understanding or my thought.

Apparently the thing we call consciousness is the strangest being in the universe, for it seems to be made of the conjunction, entailment, or perfectly intimate union of two totally different things: my act of referring and the thing to which I refer. And here is the most extraordinary part: One never realizes or discovers *a posteriori* this absolute difference between them; instead the fact of consciousness *consists* in finding something before one as distinct from and other than oneself. This table is surely not my consciousness. My present consciousness is the "table before me"; that is, the inseparable union of two such totally divergent elements as this "being before me," on the one hand, and on the other, the table.

Thus, from all the various acts of consciousness—seeing, hearing, thinking, having in mind, judging, wanting, being moved—let us select only the final residue they share: this peculiarity of always referring to something beyond themselves. And, in addition, from the things this something can be, from the targets of this referring, let us pick out the generic function common to them all, that of being what the subjective act finds before it, opposing it, as a beyond. Let us give the name "the opposed" to the least that a thing can be, to what all things are apparently forced to be or able to be, to what stands over against my act and me. In Latin "oppose" is *objicere*, and its verbal noun is *objectum*. Now we can cap our humble yet important terminological conquest with this phrase: an object is anything that can be referred to in one way or another. And the reverse: consciousness is reference to an object.

Any object, the monastery of El Escorial, for example, may stand at any one of three distances from the subject; that is, it can appear to me in three distinct forms.

First: when I am in the town of El Escorial and see the monastery, it appears to me as present. It is the monastery itself that is before me. Here we have, then, the shortest distance, that of being present.

Second: when I examine an engraving of the monastery, I have before me a piece of printed paper and not the monastery itself. But since the engraving that is present represents the monastery, this too is before me; so that by means of the engraving I still refer to it and it appears in some way within my ken. But if I analyze how the monastery is before me in contrast to its previous way of being present, I find that now it is there as absent and that all I have present is its image. Thus we have a second distance, and the form or way of absence. If you want another, clearer example, you have it in that mode of consciousness called memory; the remembered is always a past, and its remembering does not make it present (that would be absurd) but rather—here is the strange thing about memory!—it is there before us as an absence, as something past. Absence, then, is not negative in character; its character is phenomenal, immediate, as positive as pure presence and yet perfectly distinguishable from it. It is not simply a not being there, but a positive being absent and being only represented.

Reminiscences and images belong to this mode of consciousness, which has yet to be studied in detail, although various phenomenologists have been promising to do so for years. In this course I will have occasion to set forth my own research on the subject. I find this mode especially interesting because it is on this level that the plastic arts exist, and an esthetic will not be possible until we undertake the extremely difficult task of clarifying just what consciousness of the image is. Every painting, every sculpture, is an image, and every image consists of the compenetration of two objects: one present, the pigment and the lines or the volume of the marble; another absent, that is, what the pigment and the marble represent. And neither the one nor the other by itself is the work of art, but rather the two together, essentially changed and indissolubly joined.

Third distance: it would seem that, in addition to being present and absent, there is no other relation in which an object can stand to us. For example, those of you who have never seen the monastery or a reproduction of it still understood us when we spoke of this object. If we understood only what we have seen or imagined, I think we should never understand one another, for what is seen or imagined cannot itself be transferable. This transference takes place by means of signs or words.

It is a serious error to confuse understanding with knowing. When I say "infinitesimal calculus" those of you who do not know infinitesimal calculus understand me. But someone will say: in fact, I know something about it. When I hear the words "infinitesimal calculus" I say to myself: one of the disciplines or branches of mathematics. My understanding the words means that I replace them with other words. But to this pointed yet obvious observation one could oppose the following: if, in fact, the phrase "infinitesimal calculus" could be completely replaced by these—"a branch of mathematics"—and the words' comprehension, their understanding did consist in this substitution, then it is difficult to see the point of there being so many words, since if one word could always replace another, one word alone would be sufficient. Of course, this serious lack of economy may simply be a characteristic of the human race.

But the real difficulty is that the words "a branch of mathematics" are not an adequate substitute for the words "infinitesimal calculus," nor would a hundred more words be. Projective geometry is also "a branch of mathematics," and nevertheless it is not infinitesimal calculus. It is perfectly appropriate that among its countless other characteristics infinitesimal calculus be "a branch of mathematics"; but by the expression "infinitesimal calculus" we understand of course that it is not a question of just any branch, but instead precisely this unique, unmistakable one, the one we might call *h* but which we usually term "infinitesimal calculus."

The same thing happens to someone who does not know the monastery in El Escorial. He knows of other monasteries and he knows there is a town of that name in the province of Madrid; but here is the strange part—when he hears us he knows we are not referring to any of the monasteries he knows but rather to another specific, unique, exclusive, individual one, precisely the one he has not seen.

Understanding words gives us, therefore, an example of a class of conscious phenomena in which we find ourselves having to do with an object about which we know nothing, without its being present or without having a piece or a representation, an image or an emblem of it. In order to be able to acknowledge Dulcinea's matchless beauty, the merchants asked to see a portrait, even if it were only the size of a grain of wheat. Before acknowledging something they wanted to see it first and they were right. But perhaps Don Quixote wanted less, perhaps he only wanted them to understand, understand his words and the longing of his heart.

This phenomenon is indeed exasperating, and like the merchants the so-called positivists and sensationalists in psychology are angered by its not conforming docilely to their theories. For how can we possibly have consciously to do with something, be aware of something, without having any of it, without some part of it being a "content of consciousness"? "Content of consciousness" is a formidable expression, one that I have avoided using thus far, but which has now appeared on someone else's lips. We will deal with it another time and see how it is responsible for most of the sterility of contemporary psychology. It is easy to agree that the phenomenon we are dealing with is exasperating: if I were put in charge of the universe, as an act of charity to all sensationalist theories of consciousness I would do away with it. But until that happens there is no solution but to prefer the evidence of this little understood phenomenon that so perplexes questionable theories, since up until now they have failed to explain it. It may be, as Homer held, that Hector and Achilles were born to be sung by Homer; it is *not* certain that phenomena were made for theories, but the reverse.

For my part I will advance, with the necessary lack of precision that brief formulae have, the alpha and omega of my logical and methodological convictions: absolute positivism over relative positivism. All deduction, theories, and systems are true if what they say derives from direct observation of the objects themselves, of the self-same phenomena.

I cannot now see or imagine "the number containing all numbers," "the farthest star from the earth," "the first amoeba that existed"; but I do see and because I see, know, that I understand these expressions and with them refer to certain unique and unmistakable objects that are not present to me, not even as images of absent things, but instead offer themselves solely and precisely as objects I refer to and nothing more. In addition to presence and absence we have, then, the mode of reference in which the only part of the object I have is "my reference to it."

I believe we should raise again to the status of a technical *vox* our ordinary word "mention," so as to be able to describe this strange form of relation with objects— strange only according to current theories but, as we will see, the most frequent mode of consciousness. To mention something to someone does not necessarily imply that we see or imagine what is "mentioned," and yet it allows for, or at least does not preclude, the object appearing before us in a more distant or subtle way.

Let us then assume the latitude this word has in ordinary speech and use it exclusively for what perception and representation exclude. Thus we can call those acts in which the object is given us as present, perceptions or presentations; those acts when it is given as absent, representations or images; and those acts when it is given us in the mode of allusion and reference, acts of mentioning.

3 Phenomenology and Esthetics

An Essay in Esthetics
by Way of a Preface

THIS SLIM VOLUME of poems—*The Traveler*, as its author calls it—permits us to witness the appearance of a new poet and the birth of a new Muse. Poetic voices, some of them full, harmonious, or at least competent, constantly fill the air; but very few are both lyrical and new. Let us not be too severe with this lack of originality; let us apply an appropriate criticism to works of art that do not attempt to develop a new style. Let us demand fullness, harmony, and at least competence—the external virtues.

But let us reserve our love as readers for the true poets, for those men who offer a new style, who are themselves a style. These men enrich the world; they add to reality. Matter, it used to be said, neither grows nor shrinks; now physicists say that it wears away, that it diminishes. It continues to be true that it does not increase. This means that things are always the same, that no additions can be expected from matter itself. But then there is the poet who effects things like a whirlwind, who forces them into a kind of spontaneous dance. Under pressure of this virtual dynamism things acquire a new meaning; they become new things.

Matter, always old and unchanging, snatched up by whirlwinds with ever-new trajectories, is the theme of the history of art. These dynamic vortices that add novelty to the world, that add ideality to the universe, are styles.

Having reached the point, so unexpected and strange, of having to write a few pages to preface a very lovely collection of poetry, I was at a loss as to how to proceed.

The characteristic value of this book consists, as I have said, in announcing a truly new poet, a style, a Muse. On the other hand, the style, the Muse in these pages has only begun to grow. I feel it would be indelicate to approach it too soon in order to define it. I think it preferable to employ the following pages in pinning down what we mean in a general way by a poet's style, his Muse. Here the reader will sense a feeling of respect for these first words of a poet who aspires to the loftiest goal to which one can aspire in art: to be oneself.

However, the reader should be advised that in contrast to the pages of pure poetry in *The Traveler* itself, mine form a sort of dooryard of absolute prose. Mine are concerned with esthetics, a subject that is the exact opposite of art, inasmuch as it is or wishes to be a science.

I

Ruskin, the Usual, and Beauty

Reading poetry is not something I do very often. Generally speaking, I cannot conceive that reading poetry could be anyone's regular occupation. Just as we demand a certain seriousness for creating poetry, we should also demand a certain seriousness for reading it. Not a seriousness that is all show, but rather that feeling of inner awe that invades our hearts at very special times. Contemporary pedagogy is beginning to have a deplorable influence in the cultural realm of esthetics by making art a usual, normal, regulated thing. This way we lose the feeling of distance; we lose our respect for and our fear of art; we approach it at any time in the dress and mood we happen to be in, and grow accustomed to not understanding it. The real emotion to which we

refer when we sepak of esthetic pleasure these days is—
if we truly wish to own up to it—a pale delight, lacking
in vigor and depth, produced in us by the merest brush
with the work of art.

One of the men who has most dismally affected our
view of beauty is probably Ruskin, who gave art an
English interpretation. The English interpretation of
things consists in their reduction to ordinary, domestic
objects. The Englishman above all aspires to live com-
fortably and well; what sensuality is to the Frenchman
and philosophy to the German, comfort is to the Englishman. Now then, comfort and convenience require
different conditions of things, different according to the
vital function that in each case the convenience is intended to serve; only one condition is generic, inevitable,
and almost *a priori* to everything convenient—that it be
customary. It is not for nothing that England has solved
the problem of advancing without breaking with tradition. Whatever we are not accustomed to, for the sole
reason that we are not accustomed to it, makes un uncomfortable.

Ruskin manages to give an interpretation of art that
takes from art only what can easily be converted to
everyday experience. His gospel is art as usefulness and
convenience. Naturally, such a view can only recom-
mend to the intellect those arts that, to be exact, are
not really art: the industrial or decorative arts. Ruskin
insists on introducing beauty into the severe, meek English home; to do this he must first domesticate it,
weaken it, exhaust it. And so, reduced to a ghost, to an
adjective, he leads it into the honorable dwellings of
British subjects.

I am not saying that the decorative or industrial arts
are entirely without beauty; I am only saying that their
beauty is not solely beauty—it is utility varnished with

beauty, touched with beauty: water with a touch of Dionysian flavoring in it. As it happens, contemporary man has grown accustomed to not asking of art deeper emotions that those born of the decorative arts. If he were sincere he would admit that his esthetic pleasure is no different from the pleasure that derives from things when they are well tended and put in their proper order.

It would be wisdom to free the sword of beauty from that decorative sheath in which it has been kept for so long and let it flash dangerously again in the sunlight. This good twentieth century, which carries us in its strong muscular arms, seems destined to break with not a few hypocrisies and to insist on the differences that separate things. We feel something like the desire for a midday clarity rising from the roots of our souls, the enemy of a twilight vision where nothing is either black or white. Science for us will never be common sense plus the tools of measurement, nor Morality a passive honorableness in social action, nor Beauty orderliness, simplicity, or correct composition. These things—common sense, civil honorableness, orderliness—are all well and good; we have nothing against them and we would despise anyone who rejected them. But Science, Morality, and Beauty are entirely different and do not resemble these in the least. . . .

Reading poetry is not something I do very often. I need to drink water from a clean glass, but do not give me a beautiful one. In the first place, I consider it very unlikely that a drinking glass could be, in a real sense, beautiful; but if it were I could not bring it to my lips. It would seem to me that in drinking water from it, I drank the blood of a fellow human being. Either I attend to quenching my thirst or I attend to Beauty: a middle term would mean the falsification of both. So when I am thirsty please give me a glass that is full, clean, and without beauty.

There are people who have never felt thirst, what is called thirst, real thirst. And there are those who have never undergone this essential experience of Beauty. This is the only way to explain how anyone can drink from a beautiful glass.

2

The Executant "I"

We can only use or utilize things. And vice versa: things are those points at which our utilitarian activity is inserted. Now then: we can assume a utilitarian posture before all things save one, save before one solitary, one unique thing: our "I."

Kant reduces morality to his well-known formula: act so as not to use others as means, but as ends of your actions. To make these words, as Kant does, the expression of a norm and a guide in all obligations is the same as declaring that in fact each of us uses his fellow man, that we treat them as we treat things. Kant's imperative, in its various forms, would have us regard other men as *people*, not things to be used, not *things*. And this human status devolves on something when we fulfill the immortal maxim from the Gospel: treat your neighbor as yourself. Making an *I myself* of something is the only way it can cease being a thing.

But it would seem that we are allowed a choice when confronted by another person, another subject, between treating him as a thing, utilizing him, and treating him as an "I." Here there is a margin for the arbitrator, a margin that would not be possible if the other human subjects really were "I myself." The "you" and the "he" are, then, fictitiously "I." In Kant's terms we would say that my *good will* makes *you* and *he* into something like other "I's."

Earlier we spoke of the "I" as the one thing that we not only do not desire to turn, but that we cannot turn, into a thing. This is to be taken literally.

In order to see it clearly, we ought first to recall the change in meaning of a verb if it is used in the first or the third person present indicative: "I walk," for example. The meaning of *walk* in "I walk" and "he walks" evidently has a primary semblance of identity—otherwise we would not use the same verb stem. Notice that "meaning" means nothing more than "reference to an object"; therefore, "identical meaning" signifies "reference to the same object or reality, to the same aspect of some object or reality." Now then, if we direct our attention with some insistence to precisely that reality to which "I walk" alludes, we cannot help but notice how different it is from that alluded to by "he walks." His walk is a reality that I perceive with my eyes as happening in space; a series of successive positions of legs over the ground. In the "I walk" the visual image of my feet moving may occur to me; but beyond that, and as if more directly alluded to in those words, I find an invisible reality and one foreign to space—the effort, the thrust, the muscular sensations of tension and resistance. The difference could not be greater. One could say that in the "I walk" I refer to walking "seen" from inside what walking is, and in "he walks" to walking seen as an external result. However, while the relationship of walking seen as an inner event and walking as an external occurrence is self-evident, immediate, and presents itself to us without any effort on our part, this does not imply the least similarity between its two aspects. What does this peculiar thing "internal effort" or "feeling of resistance" have to do with a body changing its position in space? There is, then, an "I walk" that is completely different from "they walk."

Any other example we chose would produce the same observation. However, in cases like that of "walking" it seems the primary, the clearest meaning is the external one. Let us not become involved in finding out why this is so. It is enough if we are aware that, in contrast, there is a whole class of verbs in which the first and obvious meaning is the one expressed by the first person: "I want, I hate, I feel pain." Who has ever felt the pain or hate of anyone else? We see only contracted features or piercing eyes. What do these objects of sight have in common with what I find in myself when I feel pain or hate?

With this example, it seems to me, the distance between "I" and everything else becomes clear, whether that thing be an inanimate body or a "you" or a "he." How, in a general way, might we express this difference between the image or concept of pain and pain as felt, as hurting? Perhaps by noticing that they are mutually exclusive: the image of a pain does not hurt; moreover, it puts pain at a distance, replaces it with its ideal shadow. And vice versa: the pain hurting is the opposite of its image; in the instant that it becomes an image, it stops hurting.

"I" means, then, not this person as distinct from another, nor, even less, people as distinct from things, but rather all things—men, things, situations—inasmuch as they are occurring, being, executing themselves. Each of us is "I" according to this, not for belonging to a privileged zoological species equipped with a project-making apparatus called consciousness, but more simply because he *is* something. This red leather box that I have before me is not an "I" because it is only an image I have, and an image is exactly not what is imaged. Image, concept, etc., are always *image, concept of* . . . , and that *of which* they are an image is the real being. There is the same difference between a pain that someone tells me about and a pain that I feel as there is between the red that I see and the being red of this red leather box. *Being red* is for it what hurting is for me. Just as there is an I-John Doe, there is also an I-red, an I-water, and an I-star.

Everything, from a point of view within itself, is an "I."

Now we see why we cannot assume a utilitarian posture before the "I": simply because we cannot place ourselves *before* it, because a state of perfect interpenetration with anything is indivisible, because it is everything viewed from inside.

3
"I" and My Own I

Everything, from a point of view within itself, is an "I."

This sentence only serves as a bridge to the exact comprehension of what we are looking for. To be truthful, it is inexact.

When I feel pain, when I love or hate, I do not see my pain, nor do I see myself loving or hating. In order for me to see *my* pain, I have to interrupt being in pain and become an "I" that looks on. This "I" that observes the other one in pain is now the true "I," the executant one, the present "I." The "I" in pain, to be exact, *was*, and is now only an image, a thing or object that "I" have before me.

In this way we reach the last step in our analysis: "I" is not man in opposition to things, and not this subject in opposition to a subject "you" or "he." "I," finally, is not that "I myself," the *me ipsum* that I think

I know when I practice the Delphic saying "Know thyself." The thing I see appear on the horizon, resting briefly on the lengthened clouds of dawn like a gold amphora, is not the sun but an image of the sun; in the same way, the I that I seem to have so close at hand is only an image of my "I."

This is not the appropriate place to wage war on the original sin of the modern epoch, which like all original sins was in truth a necessary precondition for not a few virtues and triumphs. I refer to subjectivism, the mental illness of an age that began with the Renaissance, consisting of the supposition that I am what is closest to me—that is, that what is closest to me as an object of knowledge is my reality or "I" as a reality. Fichte, who before and above all else was a man of excess—excess raised to the category of genius—represents the highest intensity of this subjective fever; and a whole era came under his influence; that is, at a certain hour of the morning in all German lecture halls, the world of the "I" was produced like a handkerchief pulled from a coat pocket. After Fichte had initiated the decline of subjectivism, perhaps even now, a new way of thinking having nothing to do with subjectivism has hove into view like the faint outline of a distant coast.

The "I" my fellow citizens call John Doe, and who I am, really holds the same secrets for me as for them. And vice versa: I have no more direct knowledge of other men and things than of myself. Just as the moon shows me only a pale sidereal shoulder, so too with my "I": it is a passerby, with face hidden, that crosses my consciousness, giving me no more than a glimpse of a back draped in a Spanish cape.

Saying a thing and doing it are very different things, exclaims the common man. And Nietzsche: "It is very easy to think things; it is very difficult to be them." The distance between saying something and doing it, between thinking something and being something is exactly the same as the distance between *thing* and *I*.

4
The Esthetic Object

So we arrive at the following difficult dilemma: there is nothing we can make an object of cognition, nothing that can exist for us unless it becomes an image, a concept, an idea—unless, that is, it stops being what it is in order to become instead a shadow or outline of itself. With one thing only are we on intimate terms: our individuality, our life, but when this inwardness of ours becomes an image it too ceases to be inwardness. When I said that in "I walk" we referred to walking as seen from within, I was alluding to a relative inwardness; by comparison with the image of a body moving in space, the image of the movement of my sensations and feelings is like an inwardness. But *true inwardness, or anything in the act of executing itself*, stands at an equal distance from our image of the external and our image of the internal.

Inwardness cannot be an object for us, nor for science, nor for practical thought, nor for spontaneous representation. And nevertheless it is the true being of all things, the only sufficient thing and the only thing whose contemplation would completely satisfy us.

Let us set aside the question of whether it is rationally possible, and in what manner it would be possible, to make an object of contemplation of what appears condemned never to be an object at all. This would take us too far into metaphysical considerations. Instead let us assume an attentive frame of mind and place ourselves before a work of art—the *Pensieroso* for example, divinely calm beneath the cold light of the De Medici Chapel. And let us ask ourselves what thing it is that ultimately serves as the target, object, and subject of our contemplation.

It is not the block of marble as image of a reality: obviously, if we could hold it in memory in all its detail, its material existence would be of no importance. The consciousness of the reality of the marble body is not an element in our esthetic pleasure—or rather it is, but only as a means of arriving at an intuition of the purely imaginary object that we can then hold in its entirety in our imagination.

But neither is the imaginary object the esthetic object. There is no reason why an imaginary object should be different from a real object: the difference between them is simply that we perceive the same thing as existing or as nonexistent. But the *Pensieroso* is a new object of incomparable quality with which we come into contact by means of the imaginary object. This new object begins at the point where its images end. And it is not the whiteness of this marble, nor these lines and shapes, but rather the thing to which they allude, and which we suddenly discover before us with a presence of such fulsomeness that it can only be described as an "absolute presence."

What is the difference between the visual image that we have when we see a man thinking and the thinking of the *Pensieroso?* The visual image affects us as a narrative would; it tells us that here someone is thinking. There is still that distance between what is given us in an image and what the image refers to. But in the *Pensieroso* we have the very act of thinking executing itself. We are witness to what can never be present for us in any other way.

The description that a contemporary esthetician gives

of the very peculiar form of cognition—of knowing an object—that art affords is both trivial and erroneous. According to Lipps, I inject my "I" into the piece of polished marble, so that the inwardness of the *Pensieroso* is my own in a disguised form. This is certainly false: I am perfectly aware that the *Pensieroso* is one thing and I another, that it is its "I" and not mine.

Lipps' error derives from the subjectivistic longing to which I referred earlier; as if my "I" could ever aspire to the quite literally incomparable transparency of an esthetic object anywhere but in art. Neither in introspection nor in self-observation do I find that inwardness of thinking I find in this piece of marble. There is no more erroneous view of art than that which sees it as an underground chamber of our inner life, a means of communicating to others what flows in our spiritual depths. This is the task of language, but language merely alludes to inwardness—it never shows it.

Notice the three terms that make up every linguistic utterance. In the expression "I am in pain" we must distinguish (1) the pain itself, as felt by me, (2) my image of that pain, itself painless, and (3) the words "I am in pain." What do the sounds "I am in pain" convey to the listener, what do they mean? Not this pain of mine, but the harmless image of pain.

A narrative makes everything a ghost of itself, placing it at a distance, pushing it beyond the horizon of the here and now. What is narrated is what was, and the "was" is the schematic shape left in the present by what is absent, by what no longer is—like the discarded skin of a snake.

Now then, imagine the importance of a language or system of expressive signs whose function was not to tell us about things but to present them to us in the act of executing themselves.

Art is just such a language; this is what art does. The esthetic object is inwardness as such—it is each thing as "I."

Notice I am not saying that a work of art reveals the secret of life and of being to us; what I do say is that a work of art affords the peculiar pleasure we call esthetic by making it *seem* that the inwardness of things, their executant reality, is opened to us. By contrast, all the information offered us by science seems no more than an outline, a remote allusion, a shadow and a symbol.

5
Metaphor

When we direct our gaze at anything, it collides with the surface and rebounds, returning to our pupil. This impossibility of penetrating objects gives every cognitive act—vision, image, concept—a peculiar character of doubleness, of separation between the thing known and the person who knows. Only with transparent objects—glass, for example—does this law appear not to hold; my vision passes through glass, I pass, by means of a visual act, through the transparent body and there is a moment of interpenetration with it. In the transparent surface, the thing and I are one. But does this in fact happen? In order for the transparency of the glass to be real, I must direct my vision through it to other objects where it will rebound: a piece of glass seen against an empty background does not exist for us. The essence of glass lies in its serving as a passage to other objects: its nature is not to be itself but other things. What a strange mission of humility, of self-denial is assigned to certain beings! Woman, according to Cervantes "a transparent, beautiful glass," appears likewise condemned to being "something other than herself" in the bodily as well as the spiritual realm; woman seems destined to be a perfumed passage for other beings, allowing herself to be penetrated by both lover and child.

But to return to my point: if, instead of looking at other things through glass, I make it the end of my visual journey, then it ceases to be transparent and I find before me an opaque object.

This example of the glass can help us understand intellectually what, with perfect and simple evidence, is given us in art: an object with the double condition of being transparent and of having what is seen through it be itself, not something else.

Now then, this object that can be seen through itself, this esthetic object, is found in elementary form in metaphor. I say the esthetic object and the metaphorical object are the same, or rather that metaphor is the elementary esthetic object, the beautiful cell.

An unjustified inattention on the part of specialists has guaranteed metaphor the status of a *terra incognita*. But I am not going to attempt a theory of metaphor in this circumstantial essay; instead, I shall only suggest how a genuine esthetic object makes itself evident in metaphor.

First of all, it should be noted that the term "metaphor" means both a process and a result, a form of mental activity and the object attained through that activity.

A Valencian poet, López Picó, writes that the cypress "is like the ghost of a dead flame." This is a suggestive metaphor. But what is the metaphorical object here? It is neither the cypress, nor the flame, nor the ghost: all these belong to the realm of real images. The new object that confronts us is a "cypress-ghost of a flame." Notice, however, that this cypress is not a cypress, nor this ghost a ghost, nor this flame a flame. If we want to keep what remains of the cypress once it has been transformed into a flame, this can only be the literal identity that exists between the linear outline of both. This is the real point of resemblance between them. In every metaphor there is a true resemblance between its elements, and because of this it was thought that metaphor was essentially an assimilation, even an assimilative juxtaposition of very distant things.

This is an error. In the first place, the greater or lesser difference between things can only mean a greater or lesser resemblance between them; very distant, on these grounds, is equivalent to quite unlike. And yet metaphor satisfies us precisely because in it we find a coincidence between two things that is more profound and decisive than any mere resemblance.

And if, moreover, on reading López Picó's verse we sharpen our attention, if we insist premeditatedly on what both things in fact have in common—the linear outline of both cypress and flame—we notice that all the fascination of the metaphor vanishes, leaving us with a mute, pointless, geometrical observation. Metaphor is not, then, the mutual assimilation of real qualities.

Actually, a positive resemblance is only the first articulation of the metaphorical process. We need a real resemblance between two elements, a certain obvious proximity, but not for the purpose we suppose.

Notice that the similarities where metaphors begin are always inessential from a practical point of view. In our example the similarity of linear outline in cypress and flame is so extrinsic, so insignificant with respect to each component, that we do not hesitate to call it a pretext.

The process, then, begins with the following: the constitution of a new object called, provisionally, the "beautiful cypress" in opposition to the image of the real cypress. In order to obtain it, we must submit the latter to two operations: the first consists in freeing our selves from the visual, physical reality of the cypress by annihilating the "real" cypress; the second, in giving its image a new and very delicate quality we characterize as beauty.

In order to work the first operation, we look for something else similar to the cypress, but in some aspect unimportant to both. Then, on the basis of their inessential identity, we assert an absolute identity. Yet this is absurd, impossible. Linked together by coincidence in some insignificant aspect, the remainders of both images resist fusion and mutually repel one another. In this way, the real similarity actually serves to accentuate a real dissimilarity between them. When a real identification is evident there is no metaphor, since in the experience of metaphor there is a clear consciousness of nonidentity.

Max Müller has pointed out how in the Vedas metaphor has not evolved to the point where it uses the words "like" or "as" to express its essential ambiguity. Instead, the metaphorical operation is presented in an exposed state, stripped bare, and we can observe this early stage in the negation of identity. The poet of the Vedas does not say "firm as a rock," but *sa, parvato na acyutas—ille firmus, non rupes.* As if to say: firmness is, for the moment, solely an attribute of rocks—but he is also firm; with, therefore, a new firmness not that of rocks but new in kind. In the same way the poet offers to God his hymn *non suavem cibum,* which is sweet but not food. The sea bellows as it advances on the shore, but is not a bull.[1]

Traditional logic spoke of the mode *tollendo ponens* in which the negation of one thing is the affirmation of

1. Max Müller, *Origine et développement de la Religion,* p. 179.

another. Thus in our case the cypress-flame is not the image of a real cypress, but of a new object with something like the psychic shape of a physical tree—a shape into which a new substance, wholly foreign to the cypress, the ghostly stuff of a dead flame, flows.[2] And vice versa: the flame-image gives up its exact real outlines— which make it a flame and only a flame—so as to flow into a pure ideal shape, an imagined tendency.

The result of this first operation is the annihilation of what both objects are as practical images. When they collide with one another their hard carapaces crack and the internal matter, in a molten state, acquires the softness of plasm, ready to receive a new form and structure. The image cypress and the image flame begin to flow, to change into something about to be an ideal cypress and something about to be an ideal flame. Beyond metaphor, in extra-poetic thought, each one of the images is a terminal point for our consciousness, one of its objects. For this reason, in aiming at one of them we exclude the other. But when our metaphor makes its assertion of their fundamental identity, and with equal force an assertion of their fundamental nonidentity, we are not moved to look for this identity in what both are as real images, as objective targets. Instead, we are forced to see these as mere points of departure, raw material, signs beyond which we find their identification in a new object, in a cypress which, without absurdity, we can treat as a flame.

Second operation: even when we are aware that no identification is attributable to the real images, the metaphor continues stubbornly to suggest it to us. It pushes us

2. Actually there are three metaphors in this example: one that makes the cypress a flame, one that makes the flame a ghost, and one that makes the flame a dead flame. To simplify it I am analyzing only the first one.

into another world, where this identification is apparently possible.

A simple observation will permit us to find the way to this new world where cypresses are flames.

Every image has, in a sense, two faces. From one side it is an image of something; from the other it is, albeit an image, something of mine. I see the cypress, I have the image, I imagine the cypress. So that, with respect to the cypress, it is *only* an image; but for me it is a real state of mine, it is a moment of my "I," of my being. Naturally, while my act—seeing the cypress—is taking place, the cypress is the object that exists for me; what "I" may be at that instant is for me an unknown. On the one hand, then, "cypress" is the name of a thing; on the other, it is a verb—my seeing the cypress; if, instead, this state or activity of mine is to become an object of my perception, I will have to place myself with my back to the "real" cypress, and from there, in the opposite direction, look inward and see the cypress gradually becoming unreal, transforming itself into my activity, into my "I." In other words, I will have to find a way to force the word "cypress," with its nominal value, to become active and erupt, assuming that of a verb.

What any image is as event for my "I," as an executant state of mine, we call a feeling. Keeping this name for states of pleasure and displeasure, joy and sorrow, is an enormous error that psychology has only recently acknowledged. Every objective image, on entering or leaving our consciousness, produces a subjective reaction—just as a bird that lights on or leaves a branch starts it trembling, or turning on and off an electric current instantly produces a new current. In addition, this subjective reaction is nothing less than the act of perception itself, whether of vision, memory, or intellection. Precisely for this reason we are unaware of it; in order to attend instead to our act of vision, we would have to disregard the object before us, thereby bringing the original act to a close. Let us now return to what we were saying before: that our inwardness cannot be an unmediated object for us.

Let us return to our example. First we are invited to think of a cypress; next the cypress is removed and we are asked to place the ghost of a flame in the same ideal spot. That is, we are to see the image of a cypress through the image of a flame; we *see it as* a flame, and vice versa. But each excludes the other; they are mutually opaque. And yet it is a fact that while reading this verse we discover the possibility of a perfect fusion of the two—that is, the one, without ceasing to be what it is, can assume the same place as the other; we have, in short, a case of transparency occurring in the emotional place common to both.[3] The cypress-feeling and the flame-feeling are identical. Why? Ah! That we do not know. It is the ever-irrational fact of art, the absolute empiricism of poetry. Each metaphor marks the discovery of a law of the universe. And even when a metaphor is created we still do not know the reason for it. We simply sense an identity, we live executantly this being, the cypress-flame.

With this we leave the analysis of our example. We

3. The word "metaphor"—transference, transposition—indicates etymologically the putting of one thing in the place of another; *quasi in alieno loco collocantur,* says Cicero in *De Oratore,* III, 38. However, in metaphor the transference is always mutual: the cypress is the flame and the flame is the cypress— which suggests that the place where each of the things is put is not that of the other, but an emotional place, which is the same for both. The metaphor, then, consists of the transposition of a thing from its real place to its emotional place.

have found an object composed of three elements or dimensions: the cypress-image, the flame-image (now changed to mere properties of a third), and the emotional place, or "I" form of both. The two images endow the marvelous new body with its objective quality; its emotional value gives it the quality of depth, of inwardness. Being careful to accentuate both words equally, we might term the new object a "felt cypress."

This is the new conquest—for some a symbol of the highest reality. Thus, Carducci:

> E già che la metafora, regina
> Di nascita e conquista,
> É la sola gentil, salda, divina
> Verità che sussista . . .[4]

6
Style or the Muse

I want to add one last consideration. A nearly universal doctrine of esthetics would define art—with one set of terms or another—as the expression of human inwardness, of the individual's feelings. I am not going to dispute here an opinion that is as widespread as it is authoritative, but simply underscore the point of discrepancy between it and what is expressed in the preceding pages.

Art is not just the expression of something that existed as a reality prior to its expression. In the brief analysis of the mechanism of metaphor that I have made, emotions do not represent the terminus of the poetic task. It is false—factually false—that in a work of art a real feeling

---

4. So now metaphor, queen
   by birth and conquest,
 Is the sole wondrous, steadfast, and divine
   truth that remains.

is expressed. In our example the esthetic object is literally an *object*, the one we called a "felt cypress." So that in art feelings too are signs, expressive means; they are not what is expressed—but the stuff of a new *sui generis* corporeity. Don Quixote is not a feeling of mine, not a real person or the image of a real person: he is a new object, living in the realm of an esthetic world, a world altogether different from the physical and the psychological ones.

What happens is that the expressive function of language does no more than express in certain images (the sound or sight images of words), other images—things, people, situations, emotions—while art, in contrast, uses executant feelings as a means of expression and, in this way, gives what is expressed that executant character peculiar to it. One might say that whereas language speaks to us of things, merely alluding to them, art actualizes them. There is no reason why we should not still term art an expressive function, provided we recognize two distinct potentialities in the act of expression: an allusive one and an executant one.

If only in passing, let us deduce another important consequence with respect to what has already been said: *Art is in essence* DE-CREATION. There may be occasion in the realm of esthetics for classifying different tendencies as Idealist or Realist, but this classification must always start from the unavoidable premise that art is in essence the creation of a new object, born of the previous breakup and annihilation of real objects. As a consequence, art is doubly unreal: first, because it is not real, because it inhabits a realm that is not the one we call "real"; second, because this new and distinct thing, the esthetic object, carries the pulverization of reality within itself as one of its elements. Just as a second plane is only possible behind a first one, the territory of beauty begins on the outer edge of the real world.

In the analysis of metaphor we saw how everything depends on the use of our feelings as means of expression precisely because of what they have that is inexpressible. The mechanism for achieving this is to disturb our natural vision of things, so that by virtue of this disturbance what ordinarily passes unperceived—the emotional values of things—becomes visible.

The overcoming or breaking up of the real structure of things and their new structure or emotional interpretation are, then, two sides of the same process.

The particular manner that each poet has of de-realizing things is his style. And, looked at the other way, since this de-realization is only achieved through the subordination of the part of the image which looks toward the object to that part which is subjective, felt, or part of an "I," we can see how it can be said that the style is the man.

We must not forget that subjectivity exists only when we are concerned with things, that it only makes its appearance in the deformations we work on reality. This means that while style originates in the individuality of the "I," it is actualized in things.

The "I" of every poet is a new dictionary, a new language by virtue of which unheard-of objects—like the cypress-flame—become known to us. In the real world, we can have things before the words that allude to them; we can see them or touch them before we know their names. In the esthetic realm style is at once word, hand, and eye; only in and through style are we made aware of these new beings. And what one style says another never can. There are styles with a rich vocabulary able to quarry out innumerable, mysterious secrets; and there are styles of only three or four words, but thanks to these a corner of beauty that otherwise would have remained un-exploited comes to our attention. For this reason every true poet, bountiful or sparing, is irreplaceable. A scientist is superseded by those who follow him, but this never happens to a poet.

In addition, imitation in art is senseless. What would be the point? In science the repeatable is of value; but a style is always a unique thing.

This is why I feel a religious emotion when, on read-ing new poetry—something I only do in hours of ex-quisite, fervent superfluity—I happen on the first cries of a newborn style, the faint first smile of a new Muse, one with more than the virtues of completeness, harmony, and competence. It is a promise that the world is about to be increased.

7
The Traveler *or a New Muse*

And this is how I see Moreno Villa's book. It contains a poem entitled "The Seething Jungle" that must be read with the greatest attention. It contains nothing but poetry. It is without that minimum of reality retained by Sym-bolism in its desire to give the *impression of things*. Not even the impression is retained (as it is in the descriptive poems that precede it).

Of all physical qualities there is one in which unreality begins to appear: in fragrances. In order to perceive them we do something very like withdrawing into ourselves; we feel we have to isolate ourselves from our surround-ings, which somehow hold us and involve us in the utili-tarian sphere of real things. To appreciate a fragrance we close our eyes and take a few deep breaths so that we can be alone with it for a moment. Something on this order is required to understand the poem I mentioned, with its flesh of sweet fragrance.

From the Druidic depths of that jungle, a new Muse smiles at us; one that will grow until one day, let us hope, she reaches full maturity.

In our burning desert a rose is about to open.

Esthetics on the Streetcar

To ASK A Spaniard who has just entered a streetcar not to direct his specialist's gaze over all the women travelers is to ask the impossible. This is one of the most deeply ingrained and characteristic habits of our nation. To foreigners and to some of our compatriots this insistent, almost tactile way Spaniards have of looking at women seems impolite. I am one of these compatriots; I find it repugnant. And nevertheless I feel this custom, without the insistence, petulance, and visual tactility that usually accompany it, to be one of the most original, lovely, and generous characteristics of our race. What is true of this one is true of other manifestations of Spanish originality; as they are now, contaminated, coarse, with the rough and the smooth mixed together, they seem somehow barbaric. But if they could be purified, their exquisiteness separated from what is gross and their nobility raised to its full potential, they might well constitute a system of absolutely original mannerisms, worthy of competing with the gestural styles of the gentleman or the *homme de bonne compagnie*. The artists, poets, and men of the world have a duty to submit the brute matter of these ageless habits to the chemistry of reflective purification. That is what Velázquez did and you may be sure that the perfect stylization with which he captured Spanish gestures plays no small part in the admiration other nations feel for his work. Hermann Cohen told me that he always took advantage of his stays in Paris to go to the synagogue just to observe the gestures of the Jews who had come from Spain.

But it is not my purpose here to uncover the noble meaning that may be hidden behind the atrocious glances of Spaniards at women. This would be an interesting study for *The Spectator* who has lived for more than a few years under the influence of Plato, master of the science of looking. But my present purpose lies in another direction. Today I have taken the streetcar and since I hold that nothing Spanish is foreign to me I have activated that specialist's gaze I mentioned above. I have tried to hold in check its insistence, petulance, and tactility, and have been very surprised to discover that it has taken less than three seconds to esthetically "place" the eight or nine women riding on this conveyance and to pass firm judgment on each of them. This one is very lovely, that one less so, the one over there absolutely ugly, and so forth. Language has not sufficient terms to express all the nuances of an esthetic judgment that took place in the rapid darting of a single glance.

Since the trip was a long one and none of the ladies seemed to offer the possibility of an amorous adventure, I was obliged to begin meditating with no other object than my glance and its automatic judgments.

What is the nature—I asked myself—of this psychological phenomenon we might well call a *calculus of feminine beauty?* I am not in the least bit interested in what secret mechanism of consciousness causes and regulates this act of esthetic valuation. I am content to describe just what it is we are aware of when we do this calculus.

Psychology used to hold that the individual has a prior ideal of beauty—in this case an ideal of the feminine face that he superimposes on the real face he is looking at. Esthetic judgment would then consist simply in the perception of a coincidence or discrepancy between one and the other. This theory, derived from Plato's metaphysics, has become ingrained in esthetics and has brought along its own original error. The ideal, like the Idea in Plato, is a pre-existing unit of measurement, separate from the realities to which we apply it.

Such a theory is a construction, a typical invention of that brilliant Hellenic longing for *unity*. For to find the true God of Greece, one must go not to Olympus, a kind of chateau where a society of distinguished people enjoy a pleasant life, but to this idea of the *One*. The One is the only thing that is. White things are white and women beautiful, not each by itself, but by virtue of their greater or lesser participation in the one white thing and in the one beautiful woman. Plotinus, in whom this desire for the One reached exaggerated proportions, lumps together many expressions to suggest this tragic thirst for unity that stirs in all things. Σπεύδειν, ὀρέγεσθαι πρὸς τὸ ἕν,— they hurry, then tend towards, they long for unity. Their being, he goes so far as to say, is merely τό ἰχγος τοῦ ἑνός, the trace of unity. They feel an almost Aphrodisian lust for the One. Our own Fray Luis de Leon, who platonized and plotinized in his rough cell, found the happiest expression of all: Unity is "the universal *chirping* of things."

But all this, I repeat, is a construction. There is no single and general model that real things imitate.[1] How could I apply a pre-existent shape of feminine beauty to the faces of these ladies? It would not only be a lack of gallantry on my part—it would also be false. Instead of knowing what the highest beauty of womankind is, man perpetually searches for it from youth to old age. If he only knew it beforehand!

If we knew it beforehand life would lose one of its most efficient motors and a good part of its drama. Each woman we see for the first time awakens in us the supreme hope that she is perhaps the most beautiful. And

1. "All things *imitate the same thing*, but some come closer than others." *Enneads*, VI, 2, 11.

in this play of hopes and disenchantments that swells and contracts our hearts, life rushes through an uneven but pleasant countryside. In his chapter on the nightingale Buffon tells how one of these birds reached the age of fourteen because it had never been in love. "It is clear," Buffon comments, "that love shortens our days; but at the same time it fills them too."

To continue our analysis. Since I do not find this archetype within me, this unique model of feminine beauty, it occurs to me to ask, as it has occurred to other estheticians, if perhaps there is not a plurality of models. Various types of corporeal perfection: the perfect brunette, the ideal blonde, the ingénue, the nostalgic lady, etc.

We realize at once that this hypothesis only multiplies the difficulties of the previous one. In the first place, I have no knowledge of a gallery of exemplary faces, nor can I imagine where it would come from. In the second place, within each type I find there is an infinite number of possible different beauties. Therefore, we would have to multiply the ideal types to such a degree that they would lose their generic character; and, being as great in number as the individual faces themselves, the whole point of this theory would be lost, since it too consists in *making a norm and a prototype of the One and the General* so as to be able to evaluate the singular and the various.

Nevertheless, there is something worthwhile in a doctrine that divides the single model into a plurality of models or typical examples. For what has brought on this proliferation? Without doubt our awareness that in fact when we do our calculus of feminine beauty, we never begin with a single ideal shape and then submit a real face to it, without allowing this face any say in the matter. On the contrary, we start with the face being looked at, and the face itself, according to this theory, selects from among our models the one that is to be applied to it. In this way the individual reality collaborates in our judgment of perfection instead of remaining totally passive as in the previous theory.

Now, here is an acute observation that to my mind reveals a true phenomenon of consciousness and is not a hypothetical construction. Yes, my attitude on looking at this woman is completely different from that of a judge eager to apply a pre-established code, an agreed-upon law. I know of no such law; on the contrary, I look for it in the passing face. My glance is an absolute experience. I want to learn from the face before me exactly what beauty is. Each feminine creature offers me a completely new, unknown type of beauty; my eyes move with the emotion of one who hopes for a discovery, a sudden revelation.

The expression which describes our attitude on looking for the first time at a particular woman may seem a frivolous gallantry: "Every woman is beautiful until proven otherwise." And, we might add, with a beauty we had not foreseen.

True enough, on occasion this promise of beauty is unfulfilled. I remember in this connection an anecdote that comes from the underworld of Madrid newspaper reporting. The story is told of a theater critic, dead these many years, whose vice it was to hand out praise and censure according to the money he received in return. A tenor arrived in town who was to make his debut the next day at the Royal Theater. The needy critic hurried to visit him. He spoke of his many children and small income, and they shook hands on a thousand-peseta fee. The day of the debut began without the critic having received the agreed amount. The performance began and the money had still not arrived; the first act ended, and the next, and the next. And even back at the newspaper offices the remuneration had still not arrived when the critic sat down to write. The next day, the newspaper carried his review of the opera; in it no mention was made of the tenor until the last line, which read as follows: "We forgot to say that tenor X made his debut. He is a promising artist. It remains to be seen if this promise will be fulfilled."

Sometimes, then, the promise of beauty is not fulfilled. It took me only an instant to look at the woman in the back of the trolley and judge her ugly. Let us analyze the elements of this act of adverse judgment. In order to do this, we must repeat it more slowly. In this way, in reflection, we can catch our spontaneous consciousness in the successive stages of its activity.

And I notice the following: my glance falls first on the whole face, on its totality, and seems to pause there; then it chooses one feature, the forehead perhaps, and begins to move along it. The line is softly curved and my spirit follows it joyfully, without discomfort, and without any inward reservations.

The sentence that best describes my state of mind at this moment would be: "This is going well." But all at once, when my glance reaches the nose, I notice a kind of difficulty, an uncertainty, an obstacle. Something like what we experience when we come to a fork in the road. The downward trajectory of the forehead seems—I don't know why—as though it *ought* to be continued by the line of a different nose than the one really there. But the nose that *is* there forces my glance to follow a different path. Yes, there is no doubt about it; I see two lines, one subtle and ghostly hovering above the real nose which is, to be completely honest, rather flat. Then, confronted with this duality, the mind suffers a kind of *piétinement sur place;* it doubts, it wavers, and with this uncertainty it exposes the disparity between the feature that *ought* to be there and the one that is.

Nevertheless, we do not try to remake, bit by bit, what has displeased us as part of the whole face. There is no ideal model for a nose, a mouth, or a cheek. If we analyze the facts, we notice that every ugly, though not every monstrous, feature can seem beautiful in another context.[2]

In fact as soon as we come on a defect we know how to correct it. We add some insubstantial lines that give a bit of form here; there, on the other hand, we suppress or cut off forms already in existence. I say insubstantial lines and this is no metaphor. Our mind constantly adds them where we do not find them in fact. It is well known that we cannot look at the stars at night impartially but instead pick out one and then another from among the lighted swarm. To pick out some stars is already to put certain of them in a more intense relationship with each other; in order to do this we stretch something like cobwebs between them. The incandescent points are thus tied together so as to make up an incorporeal form. This is the psychological origin of the constellations: always, when the pure night makes its dusky blueness pulsate, the eyes of pagan man look up and see Sagittarius shooting his bow, Cassiopeia getting angry, the Virgin waiting, and Orion holding up his diamond-studded shield to Taurus the bull.

Just as the group of starry points is organized into a constellation, so the real face we see radiates an ideal profile that more or less coincides with it. In the same

2. The monstrous is a biological defect and is therefore prior to the level of esthetic judgment. The opposite of "monstrous" is not "beautiful" but "normal."

movement of our mind there wells up both the perception of a corporeal being and an intimation of its ideal
perfection.

We reach, then, the conviction that the model is not
the same for all, nor even typical. Each face gives off its
unique and exclusive ideal like a mystical phosphores-
cence. When Raphael said he painted not what he saw
but *"una certa idea que mi vieni in mente,"* we must not
understand the platonic Idea that excludes the inexhaust-
ible and multiform diversity of the real. No; each thing
from birth is endowed with its own untransferable ideal.

In this way we free esthetics from academic prison
and invite it to examine the world's riches:

Laudata sii, Diversitá
della creature, sirena
del mondo.[3]

And so, from this humble streetcar, rolling along toward
Fuencarral, I send an objection to the glittering garden of
Academia.

It is love that makes me speak . . . love for the mul-
tiplicity of life which even the best of us, against our
will, have helped to belittle. Because, just as the Greeks
held that all Being is One and reduced beauty to a norm
or general model, so Kant found Goodness and Moral
Perfection in a generic, abstract imperative.

No, no; duty is *not* the same for all. Each of us carries within his own exclusive and inalienable duty. To
guide my conduct Kant offers me a criterion: that I wish
always for what another might wish for. But this empties
the ideal. It makes it a judicial mask, a mask with the

3. Praiséd be, Diversity
of all creatures, siren
of the world . . .

features of no one. I can only fully want what I want with my whole individual being.

The calculus of feminine beauty, once analyzed, serves as a key to all the other realms of valuation. As in beauty so in ethics.

We saw earlier that the individual face is at once a design for itself as well as a more or less complete realization. And so it is with morals, for I imagine I see how each person who goes by is contained in a moral outline of himself: this profile shows how this individual would be at his most perfect. Some people completely fill the contours of their possibilities with their actions; more often we fall short of this fullness through some defect, some lack, some excess. How often we find ourselves wishing a friend might do this or that because we see with extraordinary clarity that in this way their personality would be fulfilled!

Therefore, let us measure people in terms of themselves: what each is in reality against what he potentially is. "Become what you are." Here is a just imperative. . . . But what usually happens is what Mallarmé suggests so marvelously, so mysteriously, when he calls Hamlet "the latent gentleman who cannot manage to be."

This idea of finding the sublime matrix of ideals, norms, and perfection in reality's unlimited capacity for innovation can be fruitful everywhere.

In literary and art criticism it has immediate application: just repeat in your reading the analysis we have done in our appraisal of feminine beauty. When reading a book a tapping of pleasure or displeasure gallops along the surface of what our reading conjures up. "This is going well," we say, "this is as it should be." "This is going badly; to be perfect it ought to have been otherwise." And automatically, inscribed in the work, or circum-

scribing it as we read along, we leave a critical needle-
point that is the design the work ought to have followed.
Yes, every book is first an intention and then a realization.
By the former we measure the latter. The work itself
gives us both its norm and its distance from the norm.
And the most absurd thing in the world is to measure
one author by another.

This lady sitting across from me . . .

"Cuatro Caminos," calls the conductor.

These words have always given me pause, because
they are a symbol of perplexity.

But the journey is over. What more can you expect
for ten *centimos*.

4 An Esthetics of Historical Reason

The Idea of Theater:
An Abbreviated View

WHAT IS theater? Theater, like man himself, is many different things that come into being and die, change and are transformed to such an extent that at first glance they seem not to resemble each other at all. The humans who were the models for Velázquez's dwarfs were men, and Alexander the Great, very likely the most magnificent *pecegao* [1] in all history, was a man. Precisely because a thing takes so many different forms we become interested in finding out if in all its variety some more or less latent structure does not subsist; one that would allow us to call the countless different individuals "Man" or the many and divergent manifestations "Theater." This structure that endures beneath its visible and concrete modifications is a thing's being. Therefore, the being of a thing is always to be found within the concrete, singular thing, covered by it, hidden, latent. This is why we have to uncover it, discover it, make the latent visible. In Greek, the word *lathein* means to be covered or hidden, and has the same root as our Spanish words *latente* and *latir* (to beat). We say the heart beats not because it pulses and stirs, but because it is visceral, hidden or latent within the body. When we manage to bring the hidden being of a thing to the light of day, we say we have ascertained its truth. Apparently to ascer-

1. Peach—this is the colloquial word with which Portuguese women describe a good-looking young man.

tain means to certify, to make the hidden manifest; and as it turns out the Greek word for truth—*alétheia*—means the same thing: "a" is the same as "dis"; thus *alétheia* means to uncover, to discover, to make something stop being latent. An inquiry into the being of theater means, then, an inquiry into its truth. And the notion that provides us with a thing's being or its truth is its Idea. We will try to arrive at an Idea of Theater, *the* Idea of Theater. Because of the extremely small amount of time at my disposal, I shall have to reduce the exposition of that Idea to a minimum, to offer you the *Idea of Theater in abbreviated form.* Here you have the explanation of my lecture's title: "The Idea of Theater: An Abbreviated View." Are you willing to talk about this subject for a while, for a short while? For a short while, but . . . in all seriousness, always seriously? Then let us begin.

Suppose the only time you had seen or spoken to someone was when he had stomach cramps, or a nervous attack, or a fever of a hundred and two. If, later, someone were to ask your opinion of him, would you feel you had the right to describe his personality and talents? Obviously not. You met him when he was not himself but a ruin of his former self. It is the fate of all reality to pass through these two states: one of plenitude or perfection and one of ruin. To borrow a splendid term from today's language of sports, one that would have made Plato wax enthusiastic—quite naturally, since he originated it!—to borrow, as I say, a sporting term, let us call this being in a state of plenitude and perfection "being in top form." And so oppose "being in top form" to "being in ruins."

Then just as it would be wrong to describe a man according to his appearance when he was ill, so the theater and every other reality ought to be described

when it is "in top form" and not on the basis of its deficient or ruined state. The former may explain and
clarify the latter, but the reverse is never true. Anyone
who has seen only bad bullfights—and almost all of
them are bad—has no idea what a bullfight is; anyone
who has never been fortunate enough to encounter a
splendidly feminine woman does not know what a real
woman is.

A ruin—from *ruere*—, that which has collapsed, fallen,
is in decline, decadent. It is a pity that everything in the
universe does not exist in a state of plenitude and perfection, but that instead the hour of ruin must inexor-
ably come, even to the most perfect things like virtue
and grace. Nothing is more melancholy, and this is why
the romantics, beginning with Poussin and Claude Lorraine, the proto-romantics, sought out ruins, planted
themselves delightedly in their midst and surrendered
their eyes to voluptuous tears. For the romantics got
drunk on melancholy; they imbibed the Port or Ma-
deira of their tears with delectation. They loved to
contemplate those landscapes wherein a broken arch
with failing strength holds up the stumps of its voussoirs
to heaven; where weeds enhance and smother poor fallen ashlars; where one sees moribund towers, beheaded
columns, broken-backed aqueducts. This is what Poussin
and Claude Lorraine had begun to paint in the seventeenth century. The romantics discovered the charm of
ruins. Emerson said that just as every plant has its parasite, so everything in the world has its lover and its poet.

In truth there *are* those who love ruins, and it is a
good thing such people exist. They are entirely right.
Because being in a ruined state is, as I said, one of the
two ways that reality has of being present to us. That
man who, with his countless thousands of *contos,* was
so powerful years ago, is today a ruined man. When we

were young we went to a city and there discovered a
marvelous woman who seemed made of pure light and
pure vibration, with smooth firm cheeks, delicately high-
lighted like beautiful pieces of ceramic. Many years later
when we stop again in that city and ask for her, a
friend answers: "Conchita! If you could only see her
now! She's a wreck!" Which does not mean that this
wreck called Conchita is not, perhaps, still a delight, but
only that she is a different *kind* of delight. The woman
who is no longer young is the one with the most delightful spirit of all. I remember when I was quite
young—I'm speaking now of the remote past; the words
must be in one of my first books—I wrote that in
women I prefer the period of the fall harvest when because they have been exposed to the summer sunlight
the grapes have managed to achieve a sublime sweetness.
I also recall the impression made on me when as an
adolescent I saw the famous actress Eleanor Duse; a tall,
wasted woman who was no longer young and who had
never been beautiful, and yet her face was still a trembling—trembling and delicate—soul, so that about her
eyes and lips there still hovered the suggestion of a
wounded bird with shot in one wing, a mien that can
only be described as the scar of a hundred wounds
caused by time and sorrow. And yet she was an en-
chanting woman! We "kids" left the theater with hearts
bathed in a faint glow, that species of ghostly flame that
is the St. Elmo's fire of adolescent love.

One whole side of reality, and especially one whole
side of things human, demands they be in ruins. At the
beginning of his brilliant *Lectures on the Philosophy of
History* Hegel remarks:

"When we look back and contemplate human history, at first we see only 'ruins.' History is change and
this change has, it seems, a negative aspect that causes

us sorrow. What depresses us about the past is seeing how even its most valuable creations, all the most beautiful in life, must always reach a final hour in History. History is a journey among the ruins of what was most eminent. History robs us of the noblest, the most beautiful creatures and things that have taken our fancy; passion and suffering have destroyed them; they were transitory. Everything seems in transit, nothing is permanent. What traveler has not felt this melancholy? Who, before the ruins of Carthage, of Palmyra, or Persepolis, of Rome, has not pondered the transitoriness of empires and of men, who has not been grieved by the fate of what in its day was the most intense, the fullest example of life?"

So says Hegel, who was clearly a fine writer and a very romantic one into the bargain.

But change has another aspect when viewed from its reverse side, ruin: The fact that some things end is a condition for other things being born. If buildings did not crumble in ruins, if they remained intact, there would be no place on earth today for us to live or build. We cannot, then, be content to weep among ruins; they are necessary. Man, the master builder, is the master destroyer; he could not progress if he were not also a great builder of ruins.

It is all very well for us to be romantic at times and give ourselves over to the sentimental sport of weeping for the ruin of things. But if things in a ruined state affect us like tear gas, what they cannot do—and this is my point—is serve to define the being of things. For this we need, I repeat, to approach them when they are "in top form."

This warning is extremely important nowadays because at least in the West there is almost nothing that is not in ruins, and what we can see in this evil hour, in this hour of stomach cramps, may cause us to lose sight of what things are. Today almost everything in the West is a ruin, but *not*, be it understood, *because of the war*. The ruined state was there before, it already existed. The last two wars have taken place because the West was already in ruins, according to the detailed diagnosis I was able to make more than a quarter of a century ago.[2] Almost everything is in ruins, from political institutions to the theatre, not to mention our other literary genres and the arts. Painting is in ruins— Cubism is the debris; that is why Picasso's paintings have something of the tumbled-down building about them, of the corner of a Flea Market. Music is in ruins—the most recent Stravinsky is an example of musical *detritus*. Economics is in ruins—both in theory and as practiced by nations. And finally even femininity is in ruins, in a serious state of disrepair. Yes, of course it is! And to a supreme degree. What happens is that the topic I have promised to discuss is very far from this subject; otherwise, we would have subject matter for a whole season.

Therefore, as we speak now of theater we must make an effort to keep its greatest periods in mind: fifth century Athens with its thousands of tragedies and thousands of comedies, with Aeschylus, Sophocles, and Aristophanes; the end of the sixteenth and beginning of the seventeenth centuries with the English and Spanish theaters, with Ben Jonson and Shakespeare, with Lope de Vega and Calderón; and then, near the centuries' end, the French Classical theater, with Corneille's, with Racine's, and with Marivaux' plays; the German theater of Goethe and Schiller; the Venetian theater of Goldoni, and the Neapolitan *Commedia dell'Arte;* and finally, let

2. See *The Revolt of the Masses,* published in article form beginning in 1927, and *Invertebrate Spain,* 1921.

us not forget the entire nineteenth century, one of the very great centuries of theater.

We said that we must keep all this in mind as a backdrop because it represents theater *in top form,* and also because it is of this caliber of theater that we will be speaking. The "moments" of our list are specific, concrete, yet different, forms of the best theater; best not because we, that is to say I, feel obliged to promote all this but because, whatever my, or our, personal estimate, all this is no less than the entire reality of theater at its highest moments in human history. However, in addition to this illustrious and objectively exemplary backdrop we must not forget other, less illustrious, less consecrated, forms of theater, from among which theater may be reborn in spite of its present ruin. But, as I said, this subject belongs to the other lecturers who follow me and who will recount the history of theater.

One last preliminary warning: when we said we must keep in mind the theater of Aeschylus, of Shakespeare, of Calderón, etc., you are not to understand for a moment only the poetic creations of Aeschylus, Shakespeare, and Calderón, the plays those poets wrote. Not at all! That would be an injustice which, as usually happens with injustice, only serves to mask stupidity. Foolishness, to make itself respectable, invented injustice. Because to be unjust is, at least, to be something. It was not those poetic geniuses alone and without help—at least to the extent that they were only poets—who got or kept theater "in top form." This would be a clumsy abstraction. By the theater of Aeschylus, Shakespeare, and Calderón you are to understand, as well and without possible separation from the poetic works, the actors who played them, the stages where they were performed, and the audiences who saw them.

Theater!

There is perhaps no word in our language without several meanings; most of them have many. From among these meanings linguists usually select one they call the *strong* meaning or sense of a word. This *strong* meaning is always the most precise, the strongest, the most concrete; we could also call it the most tangible one. We are going to talk about theater. Very well, let us start with the *strong* meaning of the word. Accordingly, theater is first and foremost, no more, no less, a building—an edifice with a specific structure; for example, your extremely lovely San Carlos Theater that looks as if Lisbon's *bairro Alto* carried it under its arm. However, the present use of this theater, where concerts are now given and operas sung, blurs the pure Idea of Theater. The Greeks gave another name to a theater put to these uses: they called it an *odeion*, odeum, auditorium.

On the other hand, if I were speaking to you now from the stage of the Dona María Theater, I could simply and without hesitation begin an answer to the question "What is theater?" by merely raising an arm and pointing—which is the same as saying: "Ladies and Gentlemen, theater is what you see here." But since we are not there I have asked Mr. Segurado, a draftsman, to draw me a diagram of the interior of the Dona María Theater so that I may say to you without hesitation, except that we have only a diagram of it: there you have what theater is. By a coincidence, as happy as it is unintentional, it turns out that today is the hundredth anniversary of the Dona María Theater, the most traditional and dignified in all Lisbon.

We should not despise this humblest meaning of the word, the most frequently used in everyday speech and the one with the greatest effect in the life of each of us. If we were to pass over this primary meaning of the-

ater—I repeat, the simplest, most trivial, the most readily
to hand, to wit: *that theater is a building*—we would
risk missing the rest of the reality of theater, its most
sublime, most profound, most substantial part.

By setting out from this architectural diagram of
the Dona María Theater, we are going to see if we can
make our thinking move along a rigorously dialectical
path. Dialectical thinking means that each mental step
we take forces us to take another different one; not
just any one, not an arbitrarily-chosen next step, but a
specific one, for in our first step what we saw of the
reality that concerns us here—that is, the reality "theater"—effortlessly uncovered for us a new side or component that we had been unaware of before. It is, then,
the thing itself, the reality theater itself, that will guide
our mental steps, that will be our *lazarillo*.[3] I want to
make use of our subject, which seems an unphilosophical
one, to give the young intellectuals of Lisbon an example of the most rigorous dialectical—and, at the same
time, phenomenological—method, if by chance there
are any young intellectuals here and they are not all at
the Brasileira.[4]

Theater is a building. A building is an enclosed space,
that is, one separated from the rest of space outside.
Architecture's mission is to construct an 'inside" against

3. The famous "dialectic" invented by Hegel is really a poor
thing. In it the "movement of the concept" proceeds mechanically
from contradiction to contradiction; that is, thinking is propelled
by a *blind* logical formalism. The "dialectical thinking" that I
employ as intellectual method and which is referred to in the
text is propelled by a *real dialectic* in which the thing itself moves
thought and forces it to coincide with the thing. What it consists
of, how it is possible, and why this new "method" is necessary
are things the reader will find explained briefly in a book, soon
to be published, entitled *The Origin of Philosophy*, and fully developed in another work, *Epilogue* . . . , that I hope will be out
by the end of this year.

4. A café where the Lisbon literary people meet.

the "outside" of planetary space. In enclosing space it produces an interior shape and this interior, spatial shape, which in-forms and organizes the construction materials of the building, is the desired goal. Thus, in every case, in the interior shape of a building we discover its purpose. This is why the interior shape of a cathedral is different from that of a railway station and both are different from the interior of a house. In each case the components of the shape are as they are and not otherwise because they serve one particular purpose. They are a means to this or that end. The elements of the spatial shape are, then, instruments, organs made to function in view of that end, and thus their function explains the building's shape. As the biologists of long ago would say, the function creates the organ. They might also have said that it explains it. And conversely, the idea of the building that the builders, that is, the state or the private individuals, together with the architect, have is like the soul of the inert, amorphous construction materials—stone, cement, iron—causing them to assume a specific architectural configuration. In the idea of theater—the building—you have a good example of what Aristotle called a soul or *entelequia*.

Now then, we have only to look for a moment at this drawing of the Dona María Theater in order to see the outstanding characteristic of its interior shape, namely that the enclosed space, the "inside" which is the theater, is itself divided in two: the hall where the audience will be and the stage where the actors will be. The space of the theater is, then, dual, an organic whole composed of two organs that function in relation to each other: the hall and the stage.

The hall is full of seats—orchestra seats and box seats. This indicates that the "hall" space is so disposed that certain people—those who are the audience—will be seated and hence do nothing but look on. On the other hand, the stage is an empty space on a higher level than the hall so that on it other people who are active and not still like the audience—so much so that they are called actors—will move about. But the curious part is that whatever the actors do on the stage they do before an audience, and when the audience leaves they leave too— that is, everything they do is done in order for the audience to see it. At this point we acquire another component of theater. To the first duality, which the plain, spatial shape of the building uncovered for us—the hall and the stage—another has been added that is human and not spatial: in the hall we have the audience; on the stage we have the actors.

This all begins to acquire a small but delightful degree of complexity when we notice that, as I have just said, those men and women who move and speak on the stage are not just anyone, but men and women we call actors and actresses; that is, they are characterized by an especially intense activity. Whereas the men and women who are the audience are characterized as such by a peculiar kind of passivity. In truth, in comparison with what we do the rest of the day, when we attend the theater and become the audience we do little or nothing; we let the actors *do things to us*—for example, make us cry, make us laugh. Apparently, theater is a combination of hyperactive and hyperpassive people. As audience, we are hyperpassive because the little we do is the least one can imagine doing: we *see*, and that, provisionally, is all we do. Of course in the theater we also hear, but as we shall see in a moment what we hear in the theater we hear as spoken *by* those we see. *Seeing*, then, is our primary and minimal task in theater. Therefore, to the two previous dualities—the spatial one of hall and stage, and the human one of audience and actors—we add a third:

the audience is in the hall *to see* and the actors are on the stage *to be seen*. With this third duality we arrive at something purely functional: seeing and being seen. Now we can offer a second definition of theater, a trifle more complete than the first, and say: theater is a building with an interior organic shape composed of two parts—hall and stage—so arranged as to serve two opposite yet connected functions: seeing and being seen.

From school onwards you will have heard it said that theater is a literary genre, one of the three great genres, mentioned in all literary textbooks as Drama or Dramaturgy along with Epic and Lyric Poetry. If you reflect a little, if you rid yourself momentarily of the mental set that this oft-repeated formula has burdened you with and attend only to the reality before the mind's eye when you think of theater, doesn't this inveterate notion of it as a literary genre and nothing more leave you a little perplexed? Because the literary is made up only of words—it is prose or verse, and no more. But theater is more than either prose or verse. Both exist outside the theater—in books, speeches, conversation, in poetry readings—but none of this is theater. Theater is not a reality that reaches us as pure words do through our hearing alone. In theater we not only hear but, *first and more importantly*, we *see*. We see the actors move and gesture, we see their costumes, we see the stage sets that mask the stage. And words reach us *from this ground of things seen*, emanating from it, spoken with a particular gesture, with a specific disguise and from a painted scene that is meant to be taken for a sevententh-century salon or the Roman Forum or a *beco de Mourarias*.[5]

---

5. Dead-end streets in the least fashionable section of Lisbon, where one really ought to hear the brilliant and lovely *fadist*, Amalia Rodriguez, sing a *fado*.

In theater words have a constitutive function, but it is a carefully specified one; I mean that it is secondary to the performance or spectacle. In essence, presence, and potential, theater is *something seen*—a spectacle; as audience we are above all spectators, and this is precisely what the Greek word θέατρον, theater, means: *miradouro*, a place to look out from (*mirador*).

We had good reason to be perplexed, then, dumfounded even, when we paused momentarily to consider the old saying that theater is a literary genre. Dumfoundedness is the effect produced by what dumfounds us, and the most serious dumfounder of all, and, unfortunately, the most common, is dumbness itself.

Dramaturgy is only secondarily and in part a literary genre, and for this reason even the part that is truly literature cannot be understood apart from what theater is as spectacle. We can read theater—as literature—at home at night with our slippers on, seated by the fire. Now then, what if once we had taken a careful look at it the most essential thing about the reality theater turned out to be our having to *leave our house* and *go* there? If the first, *strong*, common, and innocently fruitful meaning of the word theater signifies a building, the second meaning, equally strong and common, signifies the following: theater is a place *one goes to*. We often ask, "Is your excellency *going to the theater* tonight?" The theater is, in fact, just the opposite of our home: it is a place one *has to go to*. And this *going to*, which implies *leaving* our home, is as we will see in short order the essential dynamic core of that magnificent human reality we call theater.

So that theater is first of all a viewed or spectacular genre and not a literary one. Theater does not "happen" inside us, as do other literary genres—poems, novels, essays; instead it occurs outside us, we have to *leave* ourselves and our home and *go to see it*. The circus and the bullfight are also spectacles, events that we have to go see. However, we will shortly show how these two spectacles differ from theater. Naturally, to the extent that they are spectacles, the circus and the *tourada* belong to the same amusing family of theater. The circus and the bullfights, are, so to say, cousins of the theater: the circus is its cross-eyed cousin, the *tourada* its terrible one-eyed cousin.

But what do we see on the stage? Well, for example, we see the great hall of a castle—a medieval palace in northern Europe, one that affords a splendid view of a park, in fact the park of Elsinore; we see the bank of a river that flows slowly and sadly by, and trees leaning over its waters with a certain vague heaviness—birches, poplars, and a weeping willow with its branches hanging down. Isn't it true that the willow seems to be tired of being a tree? We see a tremulous girl with flowers and leaves in her hair, on her dress, in her hands, advancing pale and uncertain with eyes fixed on a distant point as though looking beyond the horizon to where there is no star; and yet there is a star, the loveliest of stars, the impossible star. She is Ophelia—mad, troubled Ophelia who is about to "descend to the river." "Descend to the river" is a euphemism the Chinese use to say something dies. This is what we see.

But no, this is not what we see! Have we then, just for a moment, seen an optical illusion? Because what we really saw was only painted canvas or cardboard; the river was not a river, but paint; the trees were not trees, but daubs of color. Ophelia was not Ophelia; she was . . . "Marianinha" Rey Colaço! [6]

6. Daughter of the illustrious premier actress of the Dona María Theatre, Sra. Amelia Rey Colaço de Robles Monteiro. "Marianinha" made her debut a few days after the evening when this lecture was given.

What is the answer? Did we see the former or the latter? What do we really and truly see on the stage before us? There is no doubt about it: there are two people on the stage: "Marianinha" and Ophelia. But we we don't see them—this is the curious part!—we don't see them as two people but as one and the same person. We are presented with "Marianinha" who represents, plays, Ophelia. That is to say, the things and people on the stage are presented to us under the guise, or with the potential, of *representing* other things and people they are not.

This is extraordinary. This common event, taking place daily in all the theaters of the world, is perhaps the strangest, most extraordinary adventure available to mankind. Is it not strange, extraordinary, literally magical, that a man and woman of Lisbon can sit today, in 1946, in the box and orchestra seats of the Dona María Theater and at the same time be there six or seven hundred years ago in foggy Denmark by a river in a park outside the king's palace, and there see this pale *fiammetta*, Ophelia, walking along with her airy step? If this isn't extraordinary and magical, I know of nothing in the world closer to being so!

Let us state this with more precision: there is "Marianinha" blindly crossing the stage, but the surprising thing is that she is there and not there—she is there only to disappear at each moment as if she had hidden and managed to have Ophelia take her place in the empty space of her exquisite body. The reality of an actress as actress consists in negating her own reality and replacing it with the character she plays. This is to *re*-present: to have the actor's presence present a being other than itself. "Marianinha" disappears as "Marianinha" because she is hidden by Ophelia. And the stage sets are hidden, covered by a park and a river in the same way. So that

what is *not* real, the unreal—Ophelia, the palace park—
has the strength, the magic potential to make what is
real disappear.

If you ever reflect on what you experience at the
theater and try to describe what you see on the stage,
you will have to say something like this: first and foremost I see Ophelia and a park; behind and as though at
one remove I see "Marianinha" and the clumsily painted
flats. You might say that reality retires upstage in order
to let the unreal pass through it, like projected light. On
the stage, then, one sees things—the stage sets—and people—the actors—with a gift for transparency. Through
them, as though a glass, other things appear.

Now we can generalize about what we have discovered and say: There are real things in the world
characterized by their ability to present us with things
other than themselves. We call things of this type images. A painting, for example, is a "real image." It is
under a yard wide and even less tall. In it, nevertheless,
we see a landscape several miles across. Isn't this magic?
That piece of land with its mountains and rivers and
city is there in an enchanted state. Contained in less than
a square yard we see several miles and instead of a canvas
daubed with color we find the Tagus, Lisbon, and Mon-
santo. The material painting hanging on the wall of our
home is constantly transforming itself into the Tagus
River, Lisbon, and its hills. The painting is an image because of this continual metamorphosis—and the theater
is metamorphosis too, a marvelous transformation.

I want you to be able to be astonished, amazed by
this admittedly trivial thing that happens to us every
day in the theater. Plato points out that knowledge is
born of this capacity for amazement, for astonishment,
for wonder at the fact that things are as they are and
just as they are.

What we see on the stage of the theater are images in the strict sense just defined: an imaginary world. And all the theater, no matter how humble, is a Mount Tabor where transfigurations are always taking place.

The stage of the Dona María Theater is always the same. It is neither very wide nor very high, and not very deep. It consists of a few boards, several walls, the most ordinary materials. Nevertheless, remember all the innumerable things that this small space and these ordinary materials have become in your presence. They have been a monastery and a shepherd's hut, a palace and a garden, the street of an ancient town and a modern city, and a drawing room. The same thing happens with the actors. The selfsame actor has been countless human beings: he has been a king and a beggar, Hamlet and Don Juan.

The stage and the actor are the physical form of a universal metaphor, and this is what theater is: visible metaphor.

But have you ever stopped to think what metaphor is? To make this clear, let us take as our example the simplest, oldest, and least aristocratic of metaphors, the one that says a girl's cheek is like a rose. Generally, the verb "to be" signals reality. If I say that snow *is* white we understand the reality snow is really the real color we call white. But what does "is" mean when I say that a girl's cheek *is* a rose?

Perhaps you recall that delightful short story by H. G. Wells called "The Man Who Could Work Miracles." One night in a London tavern two ordinary men, with more than their share of beer under their belts, are arguing away about whether or not there are miracles. One believes there are, the other that there are not. And at one point the disbeliever exclaims: "But that's like my telling this light to go out now and having it go out!'"; and just as he says this the light actually goes out. And from that moment on everything the man says, or even thinks without saying, happens, comes true. The series of adventures and troubles that this power, as magic as it is involuntary, brings makes up the rest of the story. Finally, a pursuing policeman comes so close that the man thinks: "Why doesn't that policeman go to the Devil!" And the policeman goes in fact to the Devil.

Just imagine the same thing happening to the simple lover whose imaginative powers only allow him to say that the cheek of his sweetheart is a rose—that suddenly her cheek really became a rose. What consternation! Wouldn't you imagine? The unlucky lover would be so distressed; he had not meant that, it was only a joke— the cheek's *being* a rose was a metaphor; it was not to *be* one in a real sense, but in an unreal one. This is why the commonest form of metaphor uses the expression *like* and says: the cheek *is like* a rose. This *is like* is not real being, but a being-like, a quasi-being: *it is unreality as such*.

Well and good, but then what happens when a metaphor occurs? Here is what happens: there is a real cheek and a real rose. When we work a metaphor, metamorphose or transform the cheek into a rose, the cheek must cease being a real cheek and the rose cease being a real rose. When identified in the metaphor the two realities knock against each other, annihilate each other, neutralize, de-materialize each other. The metaphor is a mental atomic bomb. The result of the destruction of these two realities is precisely that new and marvelous thing, unreality. By causing images of reality to knock together and annihilate each other we obtain prodigious figures that do not exist in any world. For example, to make up for the poverty of the old metaphor I used as an example, let me recall that beautiful one by a modern

Catalán poet. Speaking of a cypress, he says, "The cypress is like the ghost of a dead flame."

This *being like* is the sign of unreality. But it was a long time before language happened on this formula. Max Müller pointed out that in the Vedas, the religious poems of India, in part the oldest literary texts humanity has, metaphor is not yet expressed by saying that *one thing is another*, but rather by means of negation; which shows how correct I was in saying that two images of reality must negate, destroy each other, in order for unreality to be produced, to appear on the scene. In fact, Max Müller notes that when the Vedic poet wants to say that a man is as strong *as* a lion, he says *fortis non leo*— he is strong, but he is *not* a lion; or when he wishes to show that a character is as hard as rock, he will say *durus non rupes*—he is hard, but he is *not* a rock; he is good, but he is *not*, of course, a father.

Now then, the same thing happens in theater where the "as if" and the metaphor take on physical form—and thus become an ambiguous reality composed of two discrete ones—the actor's reality and the character's reality in the play, each one negating the other. What must happen is that for a while the actor ceases being the real person we know and also Hamlet ceases being the real man he was. It is imperative that neither be real and that both continually de-realize, neutralize one another, so that only the *unreal* as such remains, only something imaginary, pure phantasmagoria.

But this doubleness—this being at one and the same time reality and unreality—is an unstable element, and we are always in danger of ending up with only one of our two terms. The bad actor makes us suffer because he is unable to convince us he is Hamlet, and so instead we continue to see the unfortunate Pérez or Martínez that he happens to be. And, conversely, simple, unlet-

tered people are unable to enter this "informal," metaphorical, and unreal world. We all remember when our
aged and ingenuous peasant servant went to the theater
and then told us about it, how we realized she had
thought the events on the stage were real and had
wanted to warn the actor that if he stayed long he
would be killed.

Phantasmagoria will harden and then thrust the soul
of the spectator headlong into a hallucination if there
is the slightest chance.

Just as the eye muscles have to force the eyeball to
make an "accommodation" in order to see an object at
a certain distance, so our mind must also be able to adjust so that we can *see* this imaginary, ideal world of
theater—this unreality, this phantasmagoria. There are
those who, deficient in education like our old servant,
are incapable of it; but there are also many other causes
that produce a special blindness for phantasmagoria.

Let us recall an illustrious case. The year is about
1600. Spain and Portugal are united under the scepter of
our lord Philip III. This union did not mean Portugal
was ruled by Spain or Spain by Portugal, but that both
nations were mystically and symbolically joined in the
person of Philip III and in the magic wand of his sceptre.
There was more than a little of the metaphoric in this
transitory and extremely brief union of Spain and Portugal, just as there is something metaphoric in the pres-
sent-day *bloco*.

We are in a Castilian village, somewhere out there
in La Mancha, and we happen to be in the large kitchen
of an inn. Nearly the whole village is gathered together
because a puppeteer, Master Pedro, has just arrived and
is to give a performance of his puppet-theater. In a dark
corner of the vast room we can just make out the anach-
ronistic figure of Don Quixote, lanky, squalid, grace-

less, his eyes ablaze with the perpetual fever of inopportune heroism.

The figures of the puppet-theater recount how Don Gaiferos, the French knight, cousin of Roland and vassal of Charlemagne, freed his wife, Melisendra, a longtime prisoner of the Moors in Zaragoza. He has already managed their escape, has her seated behind him on his fine horse, and they are galloping happily toward their lovely France. But the Moors find they are gone and a great mob rushes after them. They draw closer, so close the couple are about to be overtaken! Then Cervantes tells us:

Upon seeing such a lot of Moors and hearing such a din, Don Quixote thought that it would be a good thing for him to aid the fugitives, and, rising to his feet, he cried out, "Never as long as I live and in my presence will I permit such violence to be done to so famous a knight and so bold a lover as Don Gaiferos. Halt, lowborn rabble; cease your pursuit and persecution, or otherwise ye shall do battle with me!"

With these words he drew his sword, and in one bound was beside the stage; and then with accelerated and unheard-of fury he began slashing at the Moorish puppets, knocking some of them over, beheading others, crippling this one, mangling that one. Among the many blows he dealt was one downward stroke that, if Master Pedro had not ducked and crouched, would have sliced off his head more easily than if it had been made of almond paste.

Once the moment of frenzy was past, Master Pedro made Don Quixote see the harm his tempestuous heroism had done; he showed him the bits and scraps of puppets that lay about on the floor, victims of the hallucination of his sword. And finally, with the noble assurance and habitual solemnity that men propelled by destiny have always used:

"I am now coming to believe," said Don Quixote, "that I was right in thinking, as I often have, that the enchanters who persecute me merely place figures like these in front of my eyes and then change and transform as they like. In all earnestness, gentlemen, I can assure you that everything that took place here seemed to me very real indeed, and Melisendra, Don Gaiferos, Marsilio, and Charlemagne were all their flesh-and-blood selves. That was why I became so angry. In order to fulfill the duties of my profession as knight-errant, I wished to aid and favor the fugitives, and with this in mind I did what you saw me do. If it came out wrong, it is not my fault but that of my wicked persecutors; but, nevertheless, I willingly sentence myself to pay the costs of my error, even though it did not proceed from malice. Reckon up what I owe you, Master Pedro, for those figures I have destroyed, and I will reimburse you in good Castilian currency." [Putnam translation, Viking Press.]

Here we see at work the duality with which we began —the hall and the theater stage, separated by the proscenium arch, that frontier between two worlds—the duality of the hall where we enjoy the reality that is ultimately ours, and the imaginary, phantasmagorical world of the stage. The imaginary and magical region of the stage where *unreality* is generated has a less dense atmosphere than that of the hall. The density and atmospheric pressure of reality is different in each space and, as happens with the very air we breathe, this differential between atmospheric pressures creates a current of air from the area of greater to that of lower pressure. The stage's mouth breathes in the audience's reality, draws it into its less dense realm of unreality. At times this flow of air amounts to a whirlwind.

In the humble kitchen of the Castilian inn the whirlwind of phantasmagoria blew that night, and the imaginary world of Master Pedro's puppet-theater breathed in the unstable, weightless soul of Don Quixote, *causing it to travel from the hall to the stage.* This means that Don Quixote ceased being a spectator, a part of the audience, and himself became a character in the play, at which point, that is to say *when he took it as reality*, he destroyed it as phantasmagoria. For notice if you will that according to him what really happened on the stage was that the Moors were actually pursuing the real Don Gaiferos and Melisendra, and it was the enchanters who changed real people into insignificant puppets. And off he dashed after the magic white tail of the little cardboard horse on which Melisendra was mounted—Melisendra is revery—off went the incandescent soul of Don Quixote, and with his soul his body, and with his body his arm, and with his arm the absurd but authentic and extremely sharp heroism of his sword!

Janet and other French psychopathologists were singularly lacking in insight, as were most French thinkers of the second half of the nineteenth century except Bergson; nevertheless, their influence has weighed heavily in the intellectual misfortunes of our two countries. And they used to say that this kind of madness was the result of a loss of a sense of reality. This seems to me perfectly absurd. Obviously, just the reverse is true: mental anomalies or aberrations of this kind betray a loss of a sense of *un*reality. It is as though a joke were taken not as a joke but in earnest, and we all know persons devoid of that modicum of intellectual agility which allows them to know when we are joking.

Now we come to the substantive difference between circus and bullfight on the one hand and theater on the other. The circus and the *tourada* are not phantasmagoria; they are real. In the circus there is only one theatrical element, only one actor: the divine, the prodigious clown, who is also an acrobat. And it is interesting to note in passing, although I have no intention of even broaching the subject of theater history, that clowning in combination with religious ritual (for this and other reasons I called him a "divine clown"), has everywhere been the origin of theater. As for the bullfight, here we have the only spectacle that is really a spectacle and, nevertheless, what it offers us is reality, reality itself. Nothing symbolizes this characteristic of tauromachy so well as the popular anecdote about what took place *circa* 1850 between the most famous bullfighter of the day, Curro Cúchares, and Spain's most famous actor, the romantic tragedian Isidoro Máiquez. Cúchares was having an extremely difficult time killing his bull, and the actor, from the front row, was shouting insults and abuse at him. Finally, at one point, when Cúchares found himself facing the bull not far from the section where the actor sat, the bullfighter shouted: *"Míquez* or Máiquez, down here dying is no fake the way it is in the theater!"

See how by beginning with a simple inspection of the interior configuration of the Doña María Theater, where we at once noticed the existence of two spaces, of two mutually functioning lobes or areas—the hall and the stage—we were able to expose this essential ingredient of phantasmagoria, of the release of unreality, in theater. In addition to this double space there was a corresponding duality in the people—actors and audience—and that duplication acquired its full meaning with the uncovering of a third functional duality: the spectators *see* and the actors *make themselves seen;* the latter are hyperactive and the former hyperpassive.

Now we shall see more clearly what this hyperactivity of the actor and this hyperpassivity of the audience are.

The actors may move about and speak in whatever style they choose—tragic, comic, or something in between—but they must always fulfill the essential, permanent, and inexorable condition that nothing they do or say ever be taken seriously; in other words, what they do and say is unreal, and is thus a fiction, a joke, a farce. Kierkegaard tells of a fire that broke out in a circus. The clown was given the job of warning the spectators, but they thought it was part of his act and were burned to death.

The activity of the actor, then, is precisely determined: his job is farce; this is why our language calls him a *farcer*. And correspondingly our passivity as audience consists in taking into ourselves the farce as such, or perhaps more exactly, in *leaving* our real, everyday lives for this world of farce. This is why I said a short time ago that it was essential that theater oblige us to *leave our house* and *go to it*—that is, to go *to* the unreal. There is no word in the language to express the peculiar reality we are when we are the audience, the spectators in the theater. Never mind; let us invent one and say: in the theater the actors are farcers and we, the audience, are "farced," we permit the farce to be worked on us.

Having reached this moment, the immensely rich, multiform human reality that is the entire history of theater can be seen to focus on a single point—as if it were the root and marrow of theater: farce. Before naming it we knew what it meant: it was what I characterized above as the strangest, most extraordinary, most authentically magical adventure that can happen to man. In farce man participates in an unreal, phantasmagorical world; he sees it, hears it, lives in it, but always, remember, *as* unreality, *as* phantasmagoria.

Now then, it is a fact that farce has existed for as long as man has been in existence. Before what we now call theater, throughout the long, broad millennia of primitive humanity, there were other varieties of farce that we can call pre-theater or prehistoric theater. We cannot stop to describe these forms now. If I allude to them it is only to draw this conclusion: since farce is one of the constant facts of history, farce must be an essential constituent of human life; it is no more and no less than an inescapable factor in our existence. Therefore, human life is not, and cannot be, only serious; it is and must sometimes be, if only for a while, a joke, a farce; *this is why theater exists,* and why the existence of theater is not the result of mere chance or a gradual accident. As we shall see in a minute, farce, the source of theater, turns out to be one of the sustainers of life, and in what it is as a fundamental dimension of our lives lies the ultimate reality and substance of theater, its being and its truth.

Time, the winner of every footrace, has beaten me in this cross-country exercise and will unfortunately not allow me to develop this part of the Idea of Theater with the necessary decorum, even though it is the decisive part.

Isn't it perplexing, isn't it therefore exciting, fascinating, that farce should turn out to be a constituent part of human life, that, consequently, together with his other ineluctable needs, man has to be "farced" and that to this end there are farcers? This is why theater exists; let there be no doubt about it.

Everything else concerning life is as far removed from farce as one can imagine; it is constant, oppressive seriousness.

We are life, our life, and each one his own life.[7] But what we are—a life—is not something we came by on our own, but instead something in which we already

7. I repeat here, with few changes, the formulas that I have so often used to define, that is, to make visible, the radical phenomenon that human life is. These expressions are not chance discoveries; they are technical terms even though they originate in the most common areas of everyday language. That this is their origin, that one has to look to ordinary language, and that there is not in the whole history of philosophy an adequate *terminology* with which to speak *formally* about the phenomenon of life is no accident, although it *is* an indictment of our philosophical past. But what *would* be frivolous would be to change these expressions with each exposition of this fundamental doctrine as though it were only a question of spinning out rhetorical figures.

were at the very moment we first discovered ourselves.
To live is to find oneself suddenly obliged to be, to exist,
in an unforeseen realm that is the world, where "world"
means always "our present world now." We have a certain amount of freedom to come and go in "our present
world," but we cannot choose beforehand the world we
are going to live in. It is imposed on us with specific and
inexorable outline and components, and we have to manage these things in order to be, to exist, to live in this
world just as it is. This is why in my first book (1914)
I called this world *our circumstances* (*la circumstancia*).
To live is to be obliged to be, whether we want to or
not, in accord with specific circumstances. This life, as
I said, was given us, for we did not come by it on our
own. Instead, we found ourselves in it and with it—just
like that, suddenly, without knowing why or to what
purpose. It was given us, not as something already made,
but as something to be made by each of us for himself.
In each successive moment we find ourselves obliged to
do something in order to go forward.

Life is not *something that is simply there* like a thing;
instead it is always something to do, a task, a gerund, a
faciendum. Still, if what we were to do in each moment
had already been decided for us, the task of living would
be less troublesome. But things are not that way; at each
moment many possible courses of action unfold before
us and we have no alternative but to choose, to decide
in each moment, which course will be ours in the next.
And we do so assuming the exclusive and untransferable
responsibility for it. When you leave here in a few minutes, at the doors of *O Século* each of you, whether he
wants to or not, will have to decide for and by himself
in which direction to take the first step. Yet, as the age-
old Indian book says, "wherever man places his foot he
treads a hundred paths." Every point in space and time

is a crossroad, a not knowing what to do. At the same time it is a place for decision and, therefore, of having to choose. But since life is perplexing, and since we have to choose what we will do, it forces us to understand, that is, to take careful account of our circumstances. This is the origin of all forms of knowledge—science, philosophy, "life-experience," and that knowledge of life usually called prudence and *sagesse*. We are consigned to our circumstances; we are their prisoners. Life is imprisonment in circumstantial reality. Man can end his own life, but if he lives—I repeat—he cannot choose the world in which he lives. His world is always the world here and now. In order to remain in it we must always be doing something. This is the reason for the countless tasks man has to do. Because life gives us a great deal to do. And so man prepares his food, does his job, builds houses, pays visits to the doctor, does business, does science, is patient, waits (which is to "spend time"), goes into politics, does charitable work, pretends . . . and creates . . . illusions.

Life is an all-embracing task. And in all his tasks man is pitted against his circumstances, because he is prisoner in a world he did not choose. This characteristic that everything around us has of being imposed on us, whether we wish it or not, is what we call "reality." We are condemned to perpetual prison in reality or the world. This is why life is so serious, so grave, that is, so difficult to bear, and why we are weighed down by the untransferable, continual responsibility that we have for our being, our tasks.

This is why when someone asked Baudelaire where he would prefer to live, he answered with a gesture of ill-humored dandyism that was, as we know, his religion: "Anywhere, anywhere, provided it's out of this world!"

With this Baudelaire meant something impossible.

Destiny decrees that man be forever chained to reality
and caught in a continual struggle against it. Escape is
impossible. This having to make our own way, and to
decide at each moment—by ourselves—what we are going to do, requires the continual application of main
strength. For this reason life is full of gravity. In such a
creature as man, whose lot is labor, effort, seriousness, responsibility, fatigue, and gravity, there is an imperative
need for some kind of rest. Rest from what? Isn't it
obvious? What else could it be? From living or, and it
amounts to the same thing, from "being in reality," from
being a castaway there.

This is what Baudelaire meant with his ironical phrase:
from time to time man needs to escape the real world.
We said that in an absolute sense this was impossible. But
might it not be possible in a less than absolute sense? In
order to leave this world while alive there would have to
be another world to go to.[8] And if the other world is
another reality, no matter how different it is, it will still
be *reality*, a preordained configuration, a set of hard circumstances. In order for there to be another world worth
going to, it will have to be, not another real world, but
an *unreal* one. Then inhabiting it, *being* in it, will mean
becoming unreal oneself. To do this would be effectively
to suspend life, to stop living for a while, to rest from
the weight of existence, to feel airy, ethereal, weightless,
invulnerable, irresponsible, nonexistent.

This is why life—man—has always made an effort to
add one other task to all the tasks that reality imposes on
him, the strangest and most surprising one of all, an undertaking that consists in no longer doing only those
things we take seriously. This task, this undertaking that

8. The other world of religion will not serve because to go
there you have to die and we are talking about a journey while
alive.

frees us from the rest is . . . play. While playing we do
nothing—that is, we do not really do anything. Play is
the purest of man's inventions; all the rest are more or
less imposed on him, and prefigured for him, by reality.
But the rules of play, of a game—and there is no game
without rules—create a nonexistent world. And rules are
pure human invention. God made the world, this world;
well and good, but man made chess . . . chess and all
other games. Man made, makes . . . the *other world*,
the world that is truly other, that does not exist, the world
of jokes and farce.

Play is, then, an art or technique that allows man to
suspend his status as reality's slave in order to free himself,
to escape, to *remove* himself from the world he lives in
to another, unreal world. This self-removal from real
life to an unreal, imaginary, phantasmagoric life is a *distraction*. Play is distraction. Man needs to rest from his
life and so must come in contact with, must turn to, or
empty himself, into a life beyond. This turning toward,
or pouring our being into, an unreal life beyond, is a
diversion. Distraction, diversion, are consubstantial with
human life; they are not accidental to it, not something
we can do without. And the person who seeks distractions is never frivolous; the frivolous person is the one
who says there must be no distractions. Of course, what
would be senseless is the desire to make life all distraction
and diversion, because then there would be nothing from
which to be diverted or distracted. Notice how the idea
of diversion presupposes two terms: a *terminus a quo*
and a *terminus ad quem*—that *from which* we are diverted and that *by which* we are diverted.[9]

This is why diversion is one of the supreme dimensions of culture. And it ought not to surprise us that Plato
the Athenian, the greatest creator and instructor of culture

9. See "Preface to *Meditations on Hunting*."

the world has ever known, entertained himself at the
end of his days with puns on the Greek word for culture,
παιδεία (*paideía*) and the Greek word for game, joke,
farce, παιδιά (*paidiá*), or that he should suggest, exagger-
ating ironically, that human life was play and that "the
play part of life is the best thing about it." [10] It is not
surprising that the Romans should imagine play as a God
called simply "Play," *Lusus,* the son of Bacchus and—
notice the coincidence!—founder of the Lusitanian race.

Play, the art or technique of diversion, because it is
one whole aspect of human culture, has given birth to
numerous forms of distraction, and these forms are ranked
from least to most perfect. The least perfect form is the
card game; there is bridge, for example, at which the
women of our day spend hours and hours of their time
in a continual revocation of their femininity—to the dis-
credit of the male members of the species. The most
perfect forms of escape to the other world are the fine
arts, and if I call them the most perfect kind of escapist
play, it is not to do them a conventional homage, not
because I favor what I long ago termed "cultural cant"
or feel disposed to kneel before the fine arts no matter
how fine or artistic they seem, but rather because they
manage to free us from *this* life more effectively than
anything else. While we are reading a distinguished novel
the mechanisms of our body continue to function, but
what I have called "our life" is literally and radically suspended. We feel distracted from our world and transported into the imaginary world of the novel.

Now then, the apex of those evasions that the fine
arts are, the one that most successfully has allowed man
to escape his difficult destiny, has been theater when it
was "in top form"—when, because of a correspondence
between audience, actor, episode, and dramatist, man has

10. *Laws.*

been wholly transported by the great phantasmagoria of the stage. This does not happen today; neither staging, actors, nor author are in tune with our emotional set, and the magical metamorphosis, the prodigious transfiguration does not usually take place. Our theater is not on a par with our sensibilities, and so theater is in ruins. But in the periods to which I have referred above countless generations have managed for many hours of their lives to realize man's highest goal—to be happy—through the divine *escapism* offered by farce.

So now you see how this simple diagram of the interior space of the Dona María Theater has led us to discover, in all its profundity yet in shockingly abbreviated form, the Idea of Theater; it has allowed us to define farce, that realization of the unreal and one of the strange realities in our universe; it has helped us to discover why man needs to be "farced" and therefore be a farcer. Man, the actor, becomes Hamlet; man, the spectator, becomes Hamlet's companion, shares in his life—and so the audience too is a farcer, it *leaves* its daily existence for an exceptional and imaginary one, and participates in a nonexistent world, an ultraworld; and in this sense not *only* the stage but the hall and the whole theater turn out to be phantasmagoria, ultralife.

At the end of the last century there was a professor of chemistry at the University of Madrid who was often the butt of students' jokes. At a raised table before his large classes he would set up experiments and announce with solemn innocence that, for example, when he mixed a certain chemical reagent with a liquid, he would get a blue precipitate. This would happen and then his students, with the cruelty that is so much a part of adolescence, would break into thunderous applause, as if the professor were a bullfighter who had just killed his bull. But the professor, bowing humbly at the applause, would say to his students: "Don't applaud me; don't applaud me; applaud the chemical reagent!"

In the same way, if the usual benevolence of this audience moves it to applaud now, I beg you to applaud the simple diagram, the diagram! It is finally responsible for your having been offered this overly long lecture.

Reviving the Paintings [1]

APPROPRIATELY ENOUGH, the first thing to be said is the humblest of truths. Painting is something that certain people do whereas others are involved in looking at it, copying it, criticizing or praising it, theorizing about it, selling it, or buying it to earn social status or at least enjoy pride of possession. Accordingly, painting is a vast repertoire of human actions. Beyond these, apart from these, painting, pictorial art, is nothing, since it is merely the material that allows for these actions—it is the wall bedaubed with *al fresco* colors, the wooden panels with enameled distemper colors, a canvas impasted with oils. But where painting, properly speaking, exists is in the actions that are expanded on these materials, or else in the actions that begin there, such as contemplation, pleasure, analysis, profit. This humble reminder, that painting is human activity and does not grow spontaneously on walls like mold or lichen, nor appear on canvases like a rash, is a point worth making. Painting is not, then, a way walls have of being nor even a way canvases have of being, but rather a way of being man that man sometimes adopts.

We are in the habit of calling each application of paint that goes onto a painting a brush stroke. But in fact in using this name we forget what we are saying, forget that a brush stroke is the movement of a brush in a hand governed by a particular intent that has arisen

1. Published in *Leonardo* (II, XII, Barcelona, 1946) with this explanation: "First chapter of my *Velázquez*, in preparation."

in someone's mind. We are still working the area of humble sayings, because this amounts to saying, in chuckle-headed fashion, that the daubs are on the painting because they were put there. This quality of having been put there is not abolished and, as it were, revoked once the paint is on the canvas. On the contrary, the colored marks retain their quality of having been put there, conserve forever their status as signs or traces of the human actions that engendered them. Even without its being man's explicit purpose, he can scarcely act upon any material without adding some trace of his intention to it; that is, once a physical object has been handled, to its own qualities is added that of being the sign, symbol, or symptom of a human design.

But there are operations in which we produce a material object with the deliberate and exclusive purpose that it be a sign of our intent. The work is then formally a vehicle of meaning. One of the broadest and most distinguished of man's gifts is this creation of signs, this semantic activity. In it we do what we do so there may come to another's attention the something within us that can only be communicated by means of a physical reality.

Speech is one such semantic creation. Writing is another. But, in addition, so are all the fine arts. Music and painting, no less than poetry, are substantially a labor of communication. Just as in poetry the poet says something to his fellow man, so too with a painting and a melody. But the word "say" which, for the present, helps us see paintings as a permanent dialogue between artist and viewer, only hinders us once this has been established. Because "saying," speech, is only one form of communication among many, and one with its own special characteristics. In fact, language is the most perfect instrument of communication man possesses. This perfection, admittedly a very relative one, lies in that in "saying" we not only communicate something but reveal it, declare it in such a way that there can be no question of what it is we wish to "say." To use a different formulation: language is impelled by the desire that its communicative activity not in its turn need any further interpretation. Whether or not this desire is fulfilled is of secondary importance. The important thing is that our words are animated by this generous purpose or ideal of releasing their meanings without more ado. This is what I alluded to in saying that as langauge communicates, it declares, that is, makes altogether clear what it communicates. The reason for this is simple. The verbal sign stands for a concept and the concept is clarity itself; in human terms it is the highest form of illumination. This is why only the concept and, of course, "saying," amount to a solution. All the rest is, in one way or another, an enigma, a conundrum, or a riddle.

For example, hieroglyphics are a form of communication such that we have only to open our eyes to see its configurations clearly. But these configurations appear with the added pretensions of having meanings. This meaning is not declared, patent, but, on the contrary, latent in them. The configurations function only as insinuations, suggestions, or, we might say, mute gesturings. This is why hieroglyphics require an effort of interpretation. Now painting is closer to hieroglyphics than it is to langauge. It is a passionate desire for communication, but with mute means. Plato long ago pointed out the painter's silence. All the marvelousness of painting rests on its dual condition: its will to express and its resolve to remain silent. To paint is to decide for silence, and yet this muteness is neither a privation nor a defect. It is a burden assumed because of a wish to express precisely certain things that language, of itself, can never "say." Language's advantage—free, declaratory communication—is won at the cost of grave limitations. The most serious of these is that it can only convey very general things. Whereas even the specific shade of a color is ineffable.[2]

This is why painting begins its communicative task where language leaves off and, like a spring, depresses itself in its muteness in order to be able to bounce back with the suggestion of ineffable things.

With this difference between the public, loquacious expressiveness of language and the mute, reticent expression of painting clarified, I return to my first claim that a painting exists only as a conjunction of signs whereby certain intentions are perpetuated. Thus, viewing a painting implies understanding it, discovering the intent of all its forms; or, to put it another way, contemplation of a painting is not just a matter of looking but of interpretation.

The instantaneousness with which a painting surrenders to our act of vision without demanding the least effort on our part is, paradoxically, the reason why painting in fact turns out to be the most hermetic of all the arts. The ease with which we see the material object called "a painting" reinforces our inertia, encouraging us to think there is no more we can do with it. On the other hand, when someone hears a piece of music and knows he "has not understood it," he never claims he has really "heard" it. There is in painting, then, a constitutional contradiction between the obviousness of its signs and the hiddenness of its meaning.

2. Poetry is not really language. It uses language merely as a medium in order only to transcend it and express what language *sensu stricto* cannot say. Poetry begins where efficacy of speech fails. It appears, therefore, as a new power of words that cannot be reduced to what words commonly are.

We perceive nothing of note when we confront a pictorial work unless we are first enthusiastic about, yet respectful of, this essential muteness. But our respect implies two things: first, that we expect of the painting no spontaneous, automatic declaration of its intent; and second, that because the painting "says nothing to us" in a literal sense, we never suppose that even its minutest part is not the vehicle of a very precise meaning. The delight of painting lies in its being a perpetual hiero-glyph before which we exist in a constant effort at in-terpretation, forever exchanging what we see for its intention. This is the source of that effluvium of meaning that continually flows from a canvas, a tablet, a drawing, an etching, or a fresco. In short, a painting is always waving to us.

But our reaction must be to avoid the vague and irresponsible spindrift of suggestions hovering over the painted area, and to force ourselves to attribute to the painting and to each of its parts a precise and unique meaning: its own, and not the one we may more or less plausibly feel like attributing to it. The way to achieve this is to energetically wrest the painting from that im-precise region where a work of art is usually allowed to float and to make it as what it in fact is, a fossil wherein part of a man's life has become mineralized, changed to a mere, inert "thing."

This is not just a manner of speaking but, at most, the somewhat exaggerated formula of a rigorous the-orem. Each bit of pigment is the enduring testimony of a resolve made by the painter: to place this bit of paint here instead of another. This decision is the true mean-ing of the pigment and therefore what we must learn to perceive. This is no easy task. Because a decision is not a "thing" but an act, and acts are real instances of pure

execution. Thus one must be ready to see the act of re-
solving to make a brushstroke as an *act*, that is, "in execution," as being carried out, and not in its result—the
pigment selected—which is already inert matter. To put
it another way: instead of seeing a painting we must
take a step back and "see" the painter painting. In the
footprint we must rediscover the stepping foot.

It is extremely important to be fully aware of all
there is in the resolve that leads a painter to make a simple brush stroke. To begin with there is the conviction
that this stroke is adequate to obtain a necessary effect
in the esthetic organism of the painting. But this means
that the conception of the whole painting is an active
part of the instigating resolve of each brush stroke, nour-
ishing and inspiring it. And so while each single stroke
of color is unimpeachable proof of a brush stroke it is
also, at the same time, a testimony of the larger resolve
that foresees the completed painting. *This* idea of the
painting, present and active in each of the subsequent
paint strokes, is the only one the painter is concerned to
communicate to us. Does this mean that once we have
discovered the general intention of the painting in one
brush stroke we have exhausted its meaning, and thus
need nothing more in order to understand it?

In an essay entitled "Principles of a New Philology"
which I hope to send to the printer soon, among others
I formulate two apparently antithetical laws, both of
which pertain to every utterance.[3] One is as follows:
"Every utterance is deficient"—that is, we never manage
to say entirely what we mean to say. The other law,
with a contrary sign, declares: "Every utterance is ex-
uberant"—that is, our pronouncements always *manifest*

3. This study is to be one of the chapters of my book *Dawn
of Historical Reason*. [Never published. Ed. note.]

much more than we intend and even some things we prefer to keep silent.[4] The contradictory aspect of these propositions disappears when we notice that both deficiency and excess refer formally, on the same level, to the utterance. Now an utterance is always a *wanting* to say *a certain specific thing*. This specific thing is what we never manage to say with enough sufficiency. There will always be a certain inadequateness between what is on our mind and what we in fact say.[5]

But the specific thing we decide to say has an enormous number of presuppositions that remain tacit because we feel they are as well understood by our listeners as by ourselves. No one ever says what he assumes another already knows. Every utterance occurs against a background of things "too obvious to mention," even though it lacks sense if these unmentioned things are absent from the minds of the listeners. Accordingly, the transaction of one person speaking to another can only take place within an ambience of things common to both parties, or rather, to say something implies countless other things that are not said. If we pull at the tip of what is said, we draw out with it, like roots, all that is understood to accompany it, so that although little may actually be said a great deal is made manifest, unintentionally or even contrary to our intentions.

But even more is involved here. The suppositions active in us when we say something are not only those of which we are aware. Behind this background of what is "too obvious to mention" another deeper and more decisive layer is operative, made up of those supposi-

4. Not that speech (*el decir*) says more than it says; it manifests more. To make manifest and to say are different. The sense-world is manifestly manifest and, nevertheless, it is not "said"; instead it is ineffable.

5. On this point see my "The Misery and Splendor of Translation" and "Ideas for a History of Philosophy."

tions which have such a profound and elemental character that we are unaware of them. If the speaker and
his listener are contemporaries, there is every likelihood
they share the same profound suppositions on which or
in which they "live, die, and have their being." This is
why a relative understanding is possible between contemporaries. But if the speaker and his listener—as can
happen in reading an ancient text or in contemplating a
painting—are of different epochs, comprehension is essentially problematic and requires a special, extremely
rigorous technique, one that reconstructs this whole
periphery of suppositions, some of them unspoken because too obvious, others because the speaker is unaware
he is keeping silent about them, although they influence
him to an extraordinary degree. This technique is what
we call "history," the technique of conversation and
friendship with the dead. As one might already suppose
at this point, history is only what it should be when we
manage to understand someone of a different period
better than he understood himself. Strictly speaking, all
history tries to understand an ancestor just as he understood himself, but it turns out that it cannot do this unless it lays bare the deepest level of suppositions on
which that ancestor lived and which, because they were
so obvious, he overlooked. Therefore, in order to understand him as he did himself, there is no choice but to
understand him better than this.

The laws of "deficiency" and "exuberance" pertain
in the realm of utterances, and also cover all semantic
activity and, hence, painting. Of the two laws only the
second, about the supererogatory character of all vol-
untary expression, is important here.

We could say that the meaning of a brush stroke is
exhausted when we have seen the total design the painter
imagined for his work, as present in each stroke, if

this design and the resolve to execute it had both come about by spontaneous generation and were complete in themselves. But the truth is just the opposite. The idea of the painting and the decision to paint it are only the specific concretion, here and now, of a previous mode of that man's activity: in other words, his way of assuming the occupation of painter. What he then sets out to paint is as it is, first, because he already understands this occupation in a certain way. If an art historian reads this he will think I am only saying that every painter has his appointed style. Clearly a painting is always conceived in the matrix of a specific style, within certain generic ways of painting that its creator preferred. His preferences, then, are present and active in each stroke, and since it is painted with an eye to the ruling styles of his period—these are, in turn, the result of previous pictorial experiences—this all weighs in each brush stroke like an enormous mass of real influences and must be revived if we wish truly to understand it. I have already pointed out, if only in passing, that it matters little whether a painter subscribes to one of the styles or paints outside and against them for the ruling styles to have a role in his painting. It goes without saying that the life, the being of the individual, depends on his period, but it is imperative to renounce once and for all the simplistic interpretation of this truth, to wit, the supposition that an individual always coincides with his epoch. This is not so: our independence with respect to our epoch has both a positive and negative side—it is both a coincidence and an opposition. The degree of one or the other varies greatly with different individuals. The error originates in the cliché that has us consider "great men" representatives of their period when it is all too obvious that they were just the opposite. Few other points reveal so clearly how little thought has been given to the structure of historical reality. In order to understand Velázquez we must be wary in this respect, for we are going to see if his art was not an unceasing battle *against* his century.

But to say every painter understands his occupation in a special way does not mean simply that he paints according to a particular style. It also, in a profound sense, means he regards his occupation *qua* occupation in a special way. The question of one's occupation is a serious one, because an occupation is no less than that to which we dedicate the largest and best portion of our lives. Imagine how great an accumulation of influences must act on us in order to make us decide in favor of one occupation and keep us at it! It is one of the most momentous decisions and therefore one of the most intimate and personal. It would be inconceivable, therefore, if the decision itself did not have an extremely individual profile. What happens is that "occupations" are really social models or mannequins, with the same generic, typical, topical character of everything social; we find them already existing like the institutions they are, in a society to which we belong, on display like different uniforms in a tailor's window. As we begin life we are treated to a performance featuring the priest, the soldier, the intellectual, the businessman, the painter, the thief, and the hangman. When we decide to be one of these we always do so by adapting the generic outlines of these social figures to our individual vocation. No one, unless he is an extreme example of ordinariness, wants to be a doctor in the abstract, according to the topical outline this public figure represents, but rather a doctor in a particular, unique way.

Therefore, we say very little about someone when we say he was a painter. We must immediately ask ourselves: how did he understand the expression "to be a painter"? What were the precise reservations in his mind when he decided to be one? And we must try to define something even more simple and obvious: to what extent did he allow his occupation to fill the total volume of his life? All manner of degree is possible here: from mere *aficionado* to day-laborer at painting. It is especially extraordinary that Velázquez specialists have not posed this question, for it is one of the first we encounter when we try to understand him!

One of the greatest influences on a painter's style is the way he views his occupation. Therefore, this factor is also included in the meaning of each brush stroke. But the choice of occupation according to distinctive criteria is no longer solely an artistic question. Thus far everything we have discovered in the pigment has been esthetic in nature, but now we pass out of the circle of art to the totality of a life. The occupation is chosen in view of the panorama our life affords us. We choose from among those forms of human existence our period allows as possible, or we choose, against these, a brand new invention of our own because the existing ones fail to satisfy us. The first painter was a painter because other modes of human existence were not to his liking.[6] That an individual decides to be a painter, and a specific kind of painter, depends, then, on what his period is and on what the occupation of painter means within it; but it also depends on what kind of man he is. It is simply inconceivable that art historians continue to ignore all these questions. Once they have said a man is a painter, they cleave to his painting and abandon the man. This is what I call "the attributive fallacy." We apply an attribute to a subject but then the attribute turns into a lion and gobbles up the subject without leaving a trace.

6. This theory of occupations and professions is developed in a series of articles entitled "On Careers" and in "Ideas for a History of Philosophy," mentioned above.

This is an ever-present sickness from which intellectuals suffer. My wish is to counteract this disease and so, following my teacher Mr. Chucklehead, as I always do, I ask the reader to notice that if it is correct to say a man is a painter, it is even more correct to say that the painter is a man and one not apart from being a painter, but *as* a painter, since painting is decidedly just one way of being a man. The stupid tradition that wants art in no one knows what detached and extra-vital region must be decisively destroyed. Only then can we begin to speak of art with precision and good sense, and not make the esthetic a kind of no-man's land from end to end as is customary now. A man's whole life and that of his entire period bears on the fact that he is a painter. It all lives in each brush stroke and must be revived, observed in action, in an executant state, in the act of functioning. In short, to see a painting clearly is to see it being born, to see it in a state of continual creation, and to revive it by making the artist's biography a presence for us. Only in this way can we attain the authentic reality of the painting.[7]

Even without the reasons that made me realize how

7. Keep in mind, therefore, that if we go from pigment to biography we are not moving to something external to the pigment or something that is, at most, its complement, but that rather we find the biography foreshortened in the pigment and it is here that we are treated to the former in its purest distillation. Because the pigment is the immortal trace of a whole past life. Naturally, in each brush stroke there is active only that portion of the life that has already happened up until the time the painter made it, and what the basic characteristics of that portion of life are only becomes clear when we contemplate the whole course of his existence. We will see how in Velázquez this reaches a paradoxical extreme, in that *the most essential part of his artistic intent is not clear in any of his paintings, but in the whole of his opus together with the rest of his life.* So much is this so that, anticipating one of the main and most extraordinary theses of this book, I will state the impossibility of sufficiently clarifying just who Velázquez was and what he set out to do in his work unless we give special weight to *what he did not paint.*

important in understanding a painting it was to specify
how the painter considered his occupation, art historians
ought to have discovered this in practice. A superior example is the case of three great Spanish painters—
Velázquez, Zurbarán, and Alonso Cano—who belong,
as it happens, to the same generation. How have art
historians been able to clarify the work of these three
painters without paying attention to the influence, so
clearly manifest in their work, of the different ways
each considered his occupation? Perhaps in other cases
this influence and this difference are not so obvious, but
when confronting this triumvirate of master painters the
viewer is literally overwhelmed by both facts. Here are
three men of the same era, the same nation, educated in
the same city, friends from adolescence on—and nevertheless there is an enormous difference in the way each
regarded his occupation; and as it effects their styles this
difference is decisive. In what follows we will be giving
examples of this difference. But there are not only differences in style, and beneath these, as a deeper reality,
special ways of regarding the occupation of painter;
there are also the deeper strata of changes in art itself.

It would be repetitious by anticipation to say here
all that should be said on this point, but at the same time
it seemed apposite to allude in passing to the concrete example of these three painters, so as to counteract that
deplorable tendency of the wayward reader to suppose—the Spanish reader, wild and skittish, more often
reads *against* than reads, and his lack of docility sometimes keeps him from even noticing the black print before him—to suppose that what has been said in this
introduction is "vague theory" that does not correspond
to any reality.

Of course if he becomes recalcitrant we can always

challenge him or anyone to explain a brush stroke by Velázquez without reference to what this painter's entire biography—and this implies the whole history of his era—contributes to that stroke in a direct, substantive, and not merely an oblique and covert way; we might further challenge him to select, instead of an outstanding brush stroke whose richness of meaning is manifest, one of the most ordinary and inane; for example, any of those that make up the background of his *Pablillos of Valladolid*. Here we have a series of color strokes that are not meant to depict any object at all, either real or imaginary, specific or imprecise. What they put before us is nothing at all, not even one of the elements. Neither earth, water, nor air. Clearly part of the artist's intention when he made those brush strokes was a desire to withhold from view any suggestion of figures or forms, to empty our attention of everything that is not the trickster's body. To this end he daubed the canvas with a formless, homogeneous matter in which nothing attracts or distracts; and, moreover, he used a gray that is the color of nothing, a color invented *ad hoc* in the studio for the sole purpose of realizing a precise aim of his pictorial technique: to make the figure of Pabillos stand out, especially his physical bulk—a plastic value that will soon disappear from the paintings. Even without pausing, let us notice how useless it is to characterize Velázquez' painting as Realism. For even if we admit the term has some value as regards the way the figure is painted, it will not serve for the painting itself, because the painting is not just the figure, but also the background, and this background is not only not realistic, and not even unrealistic, but rather violently and frankly anti-realistic, since its purpose is to stifle any suggestion of objects around the figure. What Velázquez wanted to do was to create a nothingness around Pabillos by surrounding him with an arbitrary invention that was a mere studio experiment.

Now then, fifty years earlier no one would have considered a canvas like this a painting, but instead work-in-progress, unfit to leave the studio. This body floating in space like a black ascension balloon could only have been a painting in embryo. The light shed by this first meaning of the brush stroke has been seriously diminished. Because now it turns out that we are not even sure if it is a brush stroke on a painting or on a sketch for a painting, whereupon the canvas begins to bombard us like a high-pressure hose with the following stream of unavoidable questions:

1. Did Velázquez consider a canvas in this state of completion a painting? To this we can answer at once with a rapid glance at his whole opus; almost all Velázquez' paintings are in one way or another, for one reason or another, what everyone would have called "unfinished paintings" a few years earlier.

2. What can have happened in the internal evolution of painting for a painter to intentionally paint "unfinished paintings"?

3. Whatever the reasons for this, it would have been impossible if part of the public had not reached the point in its artistic education of being able to *see* an "unfinished painting" as a completed one. Therefore, what can have happened in the external—social or collective—valuation of painting for this to occur? Notice the enormity of this. Like all the arts, painting begins by producing works that please the public. It is the painter who seeks out his viewers and adapts himself to their taste. Paintings are painted for human beings with human interests and needs, and all at once painting does an about-face, turns its back on the public and produces works that only make complete sense from the technical viewpoint of the painter:

as studio experiments. This means that a decisive sector of the public was willing to have the tables turned on it, willing to adapt to the preferences of the painter as technician. Without their having any idea of how extraordinary and inexplicable this was, people in the nineteenth century often called Velázquez "the painter's painter"—especially the English and the French. This good-for-nothing art, this painting for painters, would not seem strange today with our physics for physicists (a closed book to other mortals), our law for jurists (Kelsen), and our politics for politicians (professional revolutionaries), but it is difficult to imagine how this expression could have had any meaning around 1640.

4. Such a profound change cannot be explained away by considering it merely a new style. Instead, it meant that there had been a change in what people understood by painting, that this endeavor—creating it or enjoying it—had a different role and function in the general economy of life than the one it had had for previous generations. It is a basic mistake to believe that variations in the history of an art are simply variations in style, for in many instances the meaning of the art itself changes—what people believe they are doing when they practice it, or the end it serves in the economy of existence. The fact that we use the same names—poetry, painting, music—for works in all periods has hidden the substantive changes which, unless clarified, make it meaningless to speak seriously of literature, painting, and music. Poetry by Homer, Lope de Vega, and Verlaine is different not only because of a difference in styles; "writing poetry" is in fact a different occupation for each of them. Similarly, in the painting of the Altamira Caves, of Giotto, and of Velázquez, there is a greater difference in the painting as a human undertaking than in the painting as different styles. The Altamira painter practices magic

when he paints; Giotto prays *al fresco;* Velázquez paints paint itself. Of course, of the three ways of painting, the strangest, the most difficult to understand, is the last.[8] I

8. On this point, of supreme importance, since it implies the "fundamental historicization" of all concepts that refer to man, see what is said in *Ideas and Beliefs* and in the essay "Notes on Thinking: Its Theurgy and Its Demiurgy" (*Complete Works,* Vol. V). It was a great step forward when Riegl and Schmarsow, Wölflin and Wörringer, instead of presenting the history of art as a direct continuous line, saw it as a zig-zag, with each of the changes of direction signifying the beginning of a new intention in art or in the "artistic will" (*Kunstwollen*).

Thanks to this discovery we no longer consider the variations in art as progressive or regressive changes in the same technique at the service of one and the same esthetic purpose. In recognizing different "intentions in art" that appear now and again in the course of time, we realize that there is no one technique, more or less perfectly executed, but different techniques, each at the service of a specific artist purpose. This fertile idea, which in making a strict morphology of the history of art, has rendered it enormously more effective and precise, still has not moved beyond the circle of variations in style. This morphology, in fact, merely describes the typical forms of art with great precision, by sorting them into styles the way taxonomy does in botany and zoology. The morphological method originates with these natural sciences. It takes its departure from the artistic forms just as they are manifested in the work of art, it compares them, defines species and genres and sets out the stylistic types in a chronological series. But all this indicates that this approach takes an external view of the forms and does not treat their genesis nor explain why they came into being. At most it amounts to a cinematic history of art, essential as an instrument for a true history, but one that, for this very reason, remains on the threshold. This is why the idea of different *kunstwollen* does not even come near the subject I refer to in this section of the text, where I suggest that the functional variations of art be examined; that is, not *how* they paint, not if they paint these forms or others, but *why* the men of each epoch paint, and what role the occupation of painting has in the system of goals that is human life for each generation.

Only when *the reason why* men paint in a particular century is made clear can we understand a little of *why* they painted in a particular way. This is no longer only description, but explanation. The forms are no longer viewed from the outside but, on the contrary, taking a departure from their appearance, which is maintain that without any revolutionary fuss—he is a lordly figure whose very existence is incompatible with excitement—Velázquez brought about the profoundest change in painting since its beginnings in Giotto. We will presently see what this change entailed.

It is clear that changes of this moment are not events peculiar only to art, originating solely or principally in its internal evolution or in its external (social) evolution, but that instead, because they signify a variation in the place and role of one of the arts in the whole sphere of life, they belong to its total evolution. They transcend, therefore, the history of art and lead us to total history, the only one that is truly history.[9]

When speaking a moment ago of how each painter exercises his occupation in a certain way, I pointed out that this term could be understood in two ways—a trivial one according to which occupation is the same as style, and a more profound one in which what the painter exercises in a certain way is the occupation itself. At that time I purposely delayed mentioning until now a third meaning the expression has. And so, if painting changes, not merely as style, but also as a function in human life, it is clear that the status, character, and inspiration of the occupation must suffer a profound change at the same time.

5. All the preceding sections conspire to suggest we

---

their exterior, one enters them, reconstructs their genesis, is present at their conception and birth; in short, one understands them from within.

9. In "Ideas for a History of Philosophy" (*Complete Works*, VI) I show that what has been called "History of Philosophy" is neither history as such, nor about the reality "philosophy," since, properly speaking, there is only, *can* only be, "History of Men." The same would apply to the "History of Art," to the "History of Literature," which are only authentically history to the degree that they offer a perspective on the whole history of human life, individual and collective.

answer the following question: if, with Velázquez, painting changes not only its style but its human significance,
and becomes "painting for painters," how did he understand and regard his occupation? How did he feel about
his profession"? How did the public react to this way of
"being a painter"? Because, as I have said, without certain
people to accept his innovation, Velázquez could not
have existed, for it is certain that most of his public would
not have tolerated a painter of "unfinished paintings."
Envious old Carducho is not the only one, mentioning
as he does this scandalous state of affairs on almost every
page of his book; for Velázquez' whole life transpires to
the accompaniment of a decidedly ambiguous behavior
vis-à-vis his social context.

It is not my fault that this is not well known or has
never been mentioned before; rather, as we shall see, it
is as clear as day to those who are not entirely blind.
This being the case, we must rectify the usual idea of
who Velázquez was, and of what his life and work were.
It is customary and exact to characterize his works according to the repose and impassivity it permits us to
enjoy. Since, on the other hand, there is not one dramatic
episode in Velázquez' life, since he never wounded a
neighbor, and certainly not his wife—as Alonso Cano did
—since we never see him at odds with anyone or the
cause of a single disturbance, it has been decided that
there is nothing in his paintings but repose and impassivity
and therefore no struggle, ferocity, or heroism. We tend
not to notice any heroics unless, however real, they come
with a rhetorical accompaniment. We are usually blind to
a heroism that hides or effaces itself, that is mute, deaf,
and without sharp outline, but which, for that reason, is
all the more obstinate, resolute, and permanent.

All this has resulted in art historians keeping silent
about a sharp and disquieting feeling that, perforce, they

have always had about Velázquez' work. Undoubtedly his work offers us repose and impassivity, and this so decidedly that to many Velázquez' work seems "ordinary," "says nothing to them." These are the people who demand that a painter flatter them or that he feign enough interest to go for them with clenched fists or do a circus act, knocking himself out in their presence like our friend El Greco. But behind this repose and impassivity, art historians, men necessarily sensitive to these things, must have stumbled on a hinterland very different, stern, hard, implacable, infinitely disdainful, and distant in nature, such as is not found as far as I know in any other painter in the whole history of art. One understands why this guild of contemplators should not have perceived these qualities, for they are insolent, as irresponsible people always are, the least prepared to accept painting that blows gusts of disdain in their faces. Art historians have noticed this, must always have noticed it, but have not known what to do about it. It seemed to contradict the repose, tranquillity, and impassivity so obvious in his art; thus they never realized that these qualities were not gratuitous but a result the artist achieved thanks to strenuous efforts which were, for this reason, the very opposite of the result achieved.

Ingredients always have a different appearance from the complex unit in which they are submerged and in which they carry on a rear-guard action. Velázquez' repose is accomplished and sustained the hard way, thanks to a constant tension, *a ceaseless struggle against his entire century*. The toughness of Velázquez' paintings beneath that incomparably comfortable repose suggests the hardness of flexed biceps and the fierce discipline of a soldier in the breach, resolved not to give an inch or compromise in the least. And all this without the least posturing, without allowing himself the rhetorical excesses of the combatant, without announcing to the newspapers that he is going to fight, that he is already fighting, that he continues to do so, but simply by fighting day after day. In no other eminent man's life did as few things happen as in that of Velázquez; no life appears so empty and uninteresting. Nevertheless, this empty-seeming life is full of struggle as far as his art is concerned. This is why it is the most enigmatic of lives, one of the most difficult to understand that we can imagine. For this very reason it must be entered with the greatest circumspection, with a predisposition not to trust even one's own shadow, certain this ill-humored gentleman, this genius of reticence, will offer no clue to his arcane destiny; certain we will have to fall back on our own skill as detectives, aided by a special method to keep us from losing our way in the labyrinth that a human existence always is.

Notice how a veritable outpouring of vitally important questions has come to our attention with only a slight pressure on a bit of pigment. Behind the daub that lies without life on the canvas, completely given over to its mineral silence and dumbness, there rises, tense and vibrant, a whole organism of longings and renunciations, of attacks and defenses, of positive and negative influences, of beliefs and doubts—in short, the whole Velázquez living in that instant when his fingers hover over the palette as he prepares a brush stroke. Those painter's fingers—as Bellini, an Italian writer of that century said—are *dita pensosa*, meditative fingers, tremendously preoccupied, where all the electricity of an existence is concentrated, as on the brushes of a dynamo when a spark is about to jump. And this, all this, is what we must bring back to life, must see functioning, operative again, in order to be able to presume to have truly seen a brush stroke.

Although what has been said is only the briefest selec-

tion from among the many themes that one would have
to take up, and the selection itself was made for the sole
purpose of opening a crack in the hermeticism of the wayward reader, it will stand as an example of the method
followed in this book. In this example one can observe,
step by step, that these are not questions I have added
to the fact of the pigment on the canvas, that is, brought
into the account because of extrinsic reflections; instead
they all issue from it, have their place in it, and are imposed on us by the fact of the pigment itself. In becoming
a problem for us, an ambiguity, this brush stroke carried
us into a larger sphere that seemed to promise the key
to the enigma. This larger sphere was Velázquez' whole
work seen in the perspective of whether or not the "unfinished painting" was a frequent occurrence there. But
our affirmative answer only served to make a new problem of this larger sphere: around 1630 how was a painter
who painted unfinished paintings possible? And since we
have already seen from our first glance that such paintings
were possible, *but that it was not a normal, commonly
established mode of behavior in his time*, we have no alternative but to move out into the problematic nature of
Velázquez' entire life, which cannot have been usual or
easy, no matter what appearances suggest and in spite of
our traditional view of him.

We thus follow a trajectory in which each step
obliges us with dialectical necessity to take the following
one. It is a dialectic of real things, not concepts; of the
thing itself, not the *logos*. It is the dialectic of pulling on
a piece of yarn so as to unwind the ball of wool. We
want the leaf, only the leaf, but it turns out that the leaf
does not end with itself but is continued in the stem.
We have to take the stem as well. But the latter is continued in the branch that grows out of a trunk, which
in turn is supported by the roots in the ground. If we

really want to have the leaf we must take the entire tree, after first digging it up by the roots. This is the unavoidable fate of everything that is essentially part of a whole: the part is only what it is in relationship to the whole. This means that if a painting is anything more than the cloth of the canvas and the wood of the frame and the chemicals of the colors, what was said earlier must be taken literally: a painting is a fragment of a man's life and nothing else.

Taken this way, that is, in its most authentic reality, we achieve a revival of the painting that is actually the best possible way—and therefore exemplary—of looking at it. I do not mean to deprive anyone of the freedom of looking at paintings in any way he chooses; but the fact is that any other way than this is secondary and deficient.

Inevitably, the art "devotee" will exclaim that when he confronts a painting he is not at all interested in its history or its creator's history, but only in a purely esthetic contemplation of it, because "artistic values are eternal." This is cant. Today more than ever it has become usual to decorate all manner of things with the epithet "eternal," and so much so that the eternal is now dirt-cheap. In opposition to this view, which is nothing more than foolishness *a lo divino*, we ought to make clear that as far as man himself is concerned there is nothing eternal, but rather everything is transitory and corruptible; it comes one day and is gone the next, a cradle in flight toward the grave. There is no "eternal beauty" nor any "eternal truth." Man is the opposite of all this because he is essentially a person in need—in need of eternity. Of which he has only the stump. And he who is without eternity has to content himself with change, and change is the business of time. But real time is not that of the stars, a mineralized, abstract, unreal time, and one which, because it is unreal, enjoys the easy luxury of never com-

ing to an end. This chronometric time only exists if someone watches and counts it. Real time, on the other hand,
is time that in an absolute sense is used up and comes to
an end, that is really made up of numbered days; in short,
that lived time whose proper name is "history." The
exactness of this name lies in the fact that as each man lives
his time he finds vestiges in it of times that are not his,
that were lived and used up by other men, and for that
reason are called the "past." This gives human existence
the curious characteristic of not beginning in fact when
it really begins, but instead "having already begun." And
so that none may doubt this, so that none may forget
this, wherever man looks he sees a phantom of the past,
an admonishing, ghostly ruin.

So in a formal sense it is impossible to have a purely
esthetic contemplation in opposition to the historical contemplation of art. The person who believes he is employ-
ing the first unknowingly uses the second, except that he
makes do with the amount of history already in his head.
Inevitably, ever since the historical sense awoke in man
all contemplation has been obliged to adopt the optics of
history: an object in the past is seen as past, situated at
its actual distance. But the reverse is also true. The historical view of art is always also esthetic, and one ought,
then, to say that in a sense this vision implies a whole
series of esthetic "views" of the work, all corresponding
to different stages through which the work has passed.
This is precisely one of the enrichments that our promo-
tion of the revival of paintings brings with it.

The whole treasury of European art, above all its most
famous works, is now as common a sight as an attic clut-
tered with old family furniture; we have become used to
it, and as our perceptions have dulled it has ceased to be
there for us. But if we can manage to see the works in
their *statu nascendi* we will renew them; they will stand

before us with all the energy that gave them their power and grace when freshly created. Velázquez is here an extreme example because his paintings and certain qualities of his style are so familiar no one will deny that at first glance they now seem voiceless, dull, and rather *bourgeois;* whereas, when newly painted, they were just the opposite: formidable innovations, announcements of a new beginning, disquieting conquests, the results of a supreme daring. Perhaps they were *also* something that only Velázquez saw in them.